Pocket
BERLIN

TOP SIGHTS · LOCAL LIFE · MADE EASY

In This Book

QuickStart Guide

Your keys to understanding the city – we help you decide what to do and how to do it

Need to Know
Tips for a smooth trip

Neighbourhoods
What's where

Explore Berlin

The best things to see and do, neighbourhood by neighbourhood

Top Sights
Make the most of your visit

Local Life
The insider's city

The Best of Berlin

The city's highlights in handy lists to help you plan

Best Walks
See the city on foot

Berlin's Best...
The best experiences

Survival Guide

Tips and tricks for a seamless, hassle-free city experience

Getting Around
Travel like a local

Essential Information
Including where to stay

Our selection of the city's best places to eat, drink and experience:

◉ **Sights**

✖ **Eating**

● **Drinking**

✪ **Entertainment**

🔒 **Shopping**

These symbols give you the vital information for each listing:

☑ Telephone Numbers	👪 Family-Friendly
⊙ Opening Hours	🐾 Pet-Friendly
℗ Parking	🚌 Bus
⊖ Nonsmoking	⛴ Ferry
@ Internet Access	Ⓜ Metro
🛜 Wi-Fi Access	Ⓢ S-Bahn
🥗 Vegetarian Selection	Ⓤ U-Bahn
📖 English-Language Menu	🚋 Tram
	🚆 Train

Find each listing quickly on maps for each neighbourhood:

Bar Hemingway

16 ● Map p233, B2

Legend has it that Hemi self, wielding a machine ...rate this timber-pan ...tered bar during ... showpiece is a ...en by Papa ar ... town. Dress ...s.com; Hôtel Rit ... ⊙6.30pm-2a

Lonely Planet's Berlin

Lonely Planet Pocket Guides are designed to get you straight to the heart of the city.

Inside you'll find all the must-see sights, plus tips to make your visit to each one really memorable. We've split the city into easy-to-navigate neighbourhoods and provided clear maps so you'll find your way around with ease. Our expert authors have searched out the best of the city: walks, food, nightlife and shopping, to name a few. Because you want to explore, our 'Local Life' pages will take you to some of the most exciting areas to experience the real Berlin.

And of course you'll find all the practical tips you need for a smooth trip: itineraries for short visits, how to get around, and how much to tip the guy who serves you a drink at the end of a long day's exploration.

It's your guarantee of a really great experience.

Our Promise

You can trust our travel information because Lonely Planet authors visit the places we write about, each and every edition. We never accept freebies for positive coverage, so you can rely on us to tell it like it is.

QuickStart Guide 7.

Explore Berlin 21

Worth a Trip:

QuickStart Guide

Welcome to Berlin

Berlin is a bon vivant, passionately feasting on the smorgasbord of life. A contagious energy permeates its cafes, bars and clubs, while indie boutiques and progressive restaurants compete for your time with world-class museums and striking landmarks that reflect the city's riveting history. Whether it's must-sees or aimless explorations, Berlin delivers it all in one exciting and memorable package.

Spree River
CANADASTOCK/SHUTTERSTOCK ©

Berlin Top Sights

Reichstag & Government Quarter (p24)

Views are mesmerising from the dazzling glass cupola atop the Reichstag, the seat of the German parliament and the historic focal point of the re-united country's government quarter.

Brandenburg Gate (p26)

Prussian kings, Napoleon and Hitler have marched through this neo-classical royal city gate, once trapped behind the Berlin Wall and now a symbol of a reunited Germany.

Pergamonmuseum (p42)

Walk in the footsteps of Greeks, Romans and other ancient peoples whose architectural feats, showcased in this museum, attest to their astonishingly high levels of civilisation.

Neues Museum (p46)

Egyptian queen Nefertiti is the most famous resident at this top-ranked museum, beautifully reconstructed by David Chipperfield and also sheltering a feast of finds going back to prehistoric times.

Gedenkstätte Berliner Mauer (p74)

It's rather ironic that Berlin's biggest tourist attractions no longer exists. To get under the skin of the Berlin Wall mystique, build a visit to this indoor-outdoor memorial into your schedule.

Holocaust Memorial (p28)

Peter Eisenman poignantly captures the horror of the Nazi-inflicted Jewish mass murder with this vast, undulating maze of tomb-like concrete plinths.

Schloss Charlottenburg
(p98)

Prussian royals sure knew how to live it up, as you'll discover on a spin around their fancifully decorated living quarters in this grand palace attached to sweetly landscaped gardens.

Gemäldegalerie
(p56)

Rembrandt is here, Caravaggio too. Botticelli, Rubens, Vermeer – need we say more? Your spirits will soar as you gaze upon centuries' worth of masterpieces by Europe's art-world stars.

Potsdamer Platz
(p60)

A post-reunification re-interpretation of Berlin's one-time equivalent of Times Square, this cluster of hotels, offices and entertainment venues shows off the talents of such seminal contemporary architects as Helmut Jahn and Renzo Piano.

Jüdisches Museum (p62)

The 2000-year-old tale of Jews in Germany is a fascinating one, but just as powerful is the metaphorical message of Daniel Libeskind's extraordinary zinc-clad museum building.

East Side Gallery (p120)

On the longest surviving stretch of the Berlin Wall, more than a hundred international artists have translated their feelings about the barrier's demise into murals from playful to powerful.

Schloss & Park Sanssouci (p140)

It's practically impossible not to be enchanted by this rambling 18th-century palace ensemble dreamed up by King Frederick the Great, and a mere train ride away in Potsdam.

JON ARNOLD/GETTY IMAGES ©

EWAIS/SHUTTERSTOCK ©

STIFTUNG PREUSSISCHE SCHLÖSSER UND GÄRTEN BERLIN-BRANDENBURG/HANS CHRISTIAN KRASS ©

Berlin Local Life

Insider tips to help you find the real city

After checking out Berlin's top sights, experience what makes the city tick. Eclectic shopping strips, charismatic residential areas, chameleonesque neighbourhoods, neuron-destroying party quarters and even an antidote to 'boring Sundays' are all features that make up the Berliner's Berlin.

An Afternoon in the Bergmannkiez (p70)

▶ Eclectic shopping
▶ Urban oases

Wrapping around cafe-lined Bergmannstrasse, the Bergmannkiez (neighbourhood) is Kreuzberg's quieter and more bourgeois western section. After a spot of shopping, enjoy wide open spaces at an airport turned urban playground, contemplate the resilience of the human spirit at the Berlin Airlift Memorial and enjoy a beer on the hill that gave Kreuzberg its name.

Nosing Around Neukölln (p116)

▶ Vibrant creative scene
▶ Multicultural bar-hopping

Berlin's newest 'it' quarter is a shape-shifter, a dynamic and restless animal fed by an appetite for diversity and creativity. An exploration here is bound to be an eye-opener, perhaps even a glimpse into future trends. We can only provide suggestions on where to start, but give in to the local DIY spirit and you'll soon make your own discoveries.

Sundays in the Mauerpark (p130)

▶ Flea market and karaoke
▶ Coffee culture

When it comes to the Mauerpark, we have to agree with the tens of thousands of locals and visitors: this is a great place to be on a Sunday, especially a sunny one. A fabulous flea market, outrageous outdoor karaoke, barbecues and bands, all in a place once bifurcated by the Berlin Wall, create the ideal cocktail of fun and experience.

A Leisurely Saunter Through Schöneberg (p102)

▶ Cafe scene
▶ Indie boutiques

Often overshadowed by Kurfürstendamm to the west and Kreuzberg to the east, Schöneberg deserves its own spotlight. It's a largely residential but engagingly eclectic neighbourhood where greying suits rub shoulders with party-hearty

HINTERHOF/SHUTTERSTOCK ©

Fast-food restaurant near Kottbusser Tor (p106)

Flohmarkt am Mauerpark (p131)

MICHAEL TAYLOR/GETTY IMAGES ©

gays, ex-hippies and Turkish immigrants. Plenty of street cafes provide perfect people-watching perches.

Kotti Bar-Hop
(p106)

▶ Bars for all persuasions
▶ Restorative fast-food joints

It takes a nanosecond to figure out that Berlin has no shortage of libation stations. By our estimation, the vibrantly gritty area around Kottbusser Tor U-Bahn station has some of the city's best, and all are conveniently within stumbling distance of each other. No matter whether you're the beer or cocktail type, you'll find a favourite booze burrow here.

Other great places and ways to experience the city like a local:

Glamour shopping (p39)

Drinks with a View (p52)

Little Asia (p95)

Sunday Concerts (p85)

Haus Schwarzenberg (p82)

Street Food Thursday (p162)

Urban Playground (p126)

Knaackstrasse Cafe Scene (p136)

Berlin Day Planner

Day One

One day in Berlin? Follow this whirlwind itinerary to take in all the key sights. Book ahead for an early lift ride up to the dome of the **Reichstag** (p24), then snap a picture of the **Brandenburg Gate** (p26) before exploring the maze of the **Holocaust Memorial** (p28) and admiring the contemporary architecture of **Potsdamer Platz** (p60). See Berlin Wall remnants, then contemplate Cold War madness at **Checkpoint Charlie** (p65).

Pop into the Friedrichstadtpassagen for a dose of retail therapy before a late lunch at **Augustiner am Gendarmenmarkt** (p35). Pick up a chocolate treat at **Rausch Schokoladenhaus** (p38), then soak up the glory of **Gendarmenmarkt** (p35) on your way to Museum Island. Spend at least an hour marvelling at antiquities at the **Pergamonmuseum** (p42) until it's...beer o'clock! Head over to riverside **Strandbar Mitte** (p52).

Book ahead for a modern German dinner at **Katz Orange** (p82) or **Pauly Saal** (p82), perhaps wrapping up the night with a quiet cocktail at **Buck and Breck** (p83) or busting a move on the dance floor at **Clärchens Ballhaus** (p83).

Day Two

Spend a couple of hours coming to grips with what life in Berlin was like when the Wall still stood by exploring the **Gedenkstätte Berliner Mauer** (p131). Take a quick spin around the **Mauerpark** (p131), then grab a coffee at **Bonanza Coffee Heroes** (p130) and poke around the boutiques on Kastanienallee.

Have an exotic naan pizza for lunch at **W-der Imbiss** (p136), then start the afternoon paying your respects to Queen Nefertiti and other ancient treasures at the stunning **Neues Museum** (p46). Afterward, let the sights drift by on a one-hour river cruise around Museum Island before popping into the nearby **Humboldt-Box** (p49) to find out what to expect from the Prussian royal city palace that's being rebuilt opposite Museum Island. Enjoy the views over coffee on the panorama terrace of the Box's top-floor cafe.

Excellent nearby dinner options include meat-free gourmet fare at **Cookies Cream** (p36) or traditional German at Berlin's oldest restaurant, **Zur Letzten Instanz** (p52). After dinner, go bar-hopping around Kottbusser Tor, eg cocktails at **Würgeengel** (p107), wine at **Otto Rink** (p107) or a beer at **Luzia** (p107).

Short on time?
We've arranged Berlin's must-sees into these day-by-day itineraries to make sure you see the very best of the city in the time you have available.

Day Three

Day three starts at **Schloss Charlottenburg** (p99), where the Neuer Flügel (New Wing) and the palace garden are essential stops. Take the bus to Zoologischer Garten and meditate upon the futility of war at the **Kaiser-Wilhelm-Gedächtniskirche** (p90), then – assuming it's not Sunday – satisfy your shopping cravings along Kurfürstendamm and its side streets. Keep your wallet handy and drop by shopping mall **Bikini Berlin** (p97) and the KaDeWe department store, perhaps enjoying a casual lunch in its **food hall** (p96).

Spend an hour or two at the amazing Daniel Libeskind–designed **Jüdisches Museum** (p62), then head down to the wide open fields of **Tempelhofer Feld** (p71) to see how an old airport can be recycled into a sustainable park and playground. Have a break at the park's beer garden.

Dinner hotspots in this neck of the woods include **eins44** (p111) and **Industry Standard** (p117), both putting you close to the bars on Weserstrasse such as **Thelonius** (p117) and its side streets. If you want, extend the evening at **Club der Visionäre** (p112).

Day Four

There's plenty more to do in Berlin proper, but we recommend you spend the better part of the day exploring the parks and royal palaces in Potsdam, a mere 40-minute S-Bahn ride away. Buy online tickets for your favourite time slot to see **Schloss & Park Sanssouci** (p141), a rococo jewel of a palace. Afterwards, explore the surrounding park and its many smaller palaces at leisure. The **Chinesisches Haus** (p141) is a must-see.

Break for lunch at the park's **Potsdam Zur Historischen Mühle** (p141), then continue your park explorations or head to Potsdam's old town for a spin around the **Holländisches Viertel** (p143) (Dutch Quarter) and a classic German coffee-and-cake break. Otherwise head back to Berlin and chill beneath the chestnut trees at **Prater** (p137) beer garden.

For dinner, consider pulling up a stool at Prenzlauer Berg's lovely **Umami** (p136), followed by a stroll around beautiful Kollwitzplatz. Still got stamina? Turn your evening into a bar-hop, perhaps stopping at **Bryk Bar** (p138) or **Becketts Kopf** (p138) for fine cocktails.

Need to Know

For more information, see Survival Guide (p175)

Currency
Euro (€)

Language
German (English widely spoken)

Visas
Generally not required for tourist stays of up to 90 days (or at all for EU nationals); some nationalities need a Schengen visa.

Money
ATMs are widespread. Cash is king; credit cards are not widely used.

Mobile Phones
Mobile phones operate on GSM900/1800. Local SIM cards can be used in unlocked European and Australian phones. Multiband US phones also work in Germany.

Time
Clocks in Germany are set to Central European Time (GMT/UTC plus one hour). Daylight-savings time kicks in on the last Sunday in March and ends on the last Sunday in October.

Tipping
Servers 10%, bartenders 5%, taxi drivers 10%, porters €1 to €2 per bag, room cleaners €1 to €2 per day, toilet attendants €0.50.

1 Before You Go

Your Daily Budget

Budget: Less than €100
▶ Dorm bed or peer-to-peer rental: €10–30
▶ Club cover: €5–15
▶ Public-transport day pass: €7

Midrange: €100–200
▶ Private apartment or double room: €80–120
▶ Two-course dinner with wine: €25–40
▶ Guided tour: €10–20

Top end: More than €200
▶ Upmarket apartment or double in top-end hotel: from €160
▶ Gourmet two-course dinner with wine: €70
▶ Cab ride: €25

Useful Websites

Lonely Planet (www.lonelyplanet.com/germany/berlin) Destination information, hotel bookings, traveller forum and more.

Visit Berlin (www.visitberlin.de) Official tourist authority info.

Museumsportal (www.museumsportal-berlin.de) Gateway to the city's museums.

Resident Advisor (www.residentadvisor.net) Guide to parties and clubbing.

Advance Planning

Two to three months before Book tickets for the Berliner Philharmonie, the Staatsoper, Sammlung Boros and other top-flight events.

One month before Book online tickets for the Reichstag dome, the Neues Museum and the Pergamonmuseum.

Two weeks before Reserve a table at trendy or Michelin-starred restaurants, especially for Friday and Saturday dinners.

② Arriving in Berlin

Most visitors arrive at one of Berlin's two airports: Tegel or Schönefeld (www.berlin-airport.de). The Hauptbahnhof (main train station) is in the city centre, the ZOB (central coach station) in the far western city.

✈ From Berlin-Tegel Airport

Destination	Best Transport
Alexanderplatz	TXL express bus
Kurfürstendamm	X9 express bus
Kreuzberg/ Kottbusser Tor	Bus 109 to Uhland-strasse, then U1
Potsdamer Platz	X9 to Ernst-Reuter-Platz, then U2

✈ From Berlin-Schönefeld Airport

Destination	Best Transport
Alexanderplatz	Airport-Express train (RB14 or RE7), S9
Bahnhof Zoologischer Garten	Airport-Express
Kreuzberg/ Kottbusser Tor	Airport-Express to Alexanderplatz, then U8
Potsdamer Platz	Airport-Express to Friedrichstrasse, then S1, S2 or S25

🚌 From Hauptbahnhof

Berlin's central train station is served by buses, trams, and U-Bahn and S-Bahn trains.

🚌 From ZOB (Central Coach Station)

The central coach station is a short walk from both U-Bahn and S-Bahn stations.

③ Getting Around

Berlin has an extensive and fairly reliable public transport system consisting of the U-Bahn (underground, or subway), S-Bahn (light rail), buses and trams. One ticket is valid on all forms of transport. Day passes are available. Most tickets need to be validated (stamped) before or upon boarding. For trip planning, see www.bvg.de

U U-Bahn

Most efficient way to travel; operates 4am to 12.30am and all night Friday, Saturday and public holidays. From Sunday to Thursday, half-hourly night buses take over in the interim.

S S-Bahn

Less frequent than U-Bahn trains but with fewer stops and thus useful for longer distances. Same operating hours as the U-Bahn.

🚌 Bus

Slow but useful for sightseeing on the cheap. Run frequently 4.30am to 12.30am; half-hourly night buses in the interim. MetroBuses (designated M1, M19 etc) operate 24/7.

🚋 Tram

Only in the eastern districts; MetroTrams (designated M1, M2 etc) run 24/7.

☊ Cycling

Bike lanes and rental stations abound; bikes are allowed in specially marked U-Bahn and S-Bahn carriages.

🚕 Taxi

Can be hailed; fairly inexpensive. Avoid during daytime rush hour.

🚗 Uber

The only Uber option in Berlin is uberTaxi. Prices are identical to regular taxis, including a surcharge of €1.50 for cash-free payments.

Berlin Neighbourhoods

Scheunenviertel (p72)

The maze-like historic Jewish Quarter is fashionista central and also teems with hip bars and restaurants.

⊙ Top Sights

Gedenkstätte Berliner Mauer

Reichstag & Unter den Linden (p22)

Berlin's historic hub delivers great views, iconic landmarks and the city's most beautiful boulevard.

⊙ Top Sights

Reichstag & Government Quarter

Brandenburg Gate & Pariser Platz

Holocaust Memorial

Schloss Charlottenburg ⊙

Reichstag & Government Quarter ⊙

Brandenburg Gate & Pariser Platz ⊙

Holocaust Memorial ⊙

Gemäldegalerie ⊙

Potsdamer Platz

Schloss & Park Sanssouci (20km)

Worth a Trip

⊙ Top Sights

Schloss Charlottenburg

Schloss & Park Sanssouci

Kurfürstendamm (p86)

Nirvana for shopaholics, this grand boulevard spills into idyllic side streets teeming with quaint shops, bustling cafes and restaurants.

Potsdamer Platz (p54)

This brand-new quarter, on ground once bisected by the Berlin Wall, is now a showcase of fabulous contemporary architecture.

⊙ Top Sights

Gemäldegalerie

Potsdamer Platz

Jüdisches Museum

Prenzlauer Berg (p128)
This charismatic neighbourhood entices with fun shopping, gorgeous townhouses, cosy cafes and a fabulous flea market.

Museum Island & Alexanderplatz (p40)
Gawk at a pirate's chest of treasure from ancient civilisations guarded by the soaring TV Tower on socialist-styled Alexanderplatz.

⊙ Top Sights

Pergamonmuseum

Neues Museum

⊙ *Gedenkstätte Berliner Mauer*

⊙ *Pergamonmuseum*
⊙ *Neues Museum*

Jüdisches
⊙ *Museum*

⊙ *East Side Gallery*

Kreuzberg (p104)
Gritty but cool, Kreuzberg is a joy to explore on foot, with a vibrant restaurant scene and Berlin's most happening nightlife.

Friedrichshain (p118)
This student-flavoured district is tailor-made for soaking up Berlin's laid-back vibe and great for nightlife explorations.

⊙ Top Sights

East Side Gallery

Explore
Berlin

Worth a Trip

Paul-Löbe-Haus (p25)
©BY FELDMAN_1/GETTY IMAGES ©

Explore

Reichstag & Unter den Linden

It's been burned, bombed, rebuilt, buttressed by the Berlin Wall, wrapped in fabric and, finally, adorned with a glass dome: this is the Reichstag, one of Berlin's most iconic buildings and seat of the German parliament (Bundestag). Nearby, the Brandenburg Gate gives way to Unter den Linden, Berlin's most elegant boulevard, which flaunts its Prussian pedigree with pride.

MBIRD/BY GETTY IMAGES ©

The Sights in a Day

☀ Book an early time slot for the lift ride to the **Reichstag** (p24) dome and get the lay of the land while meandering up its spiralling ramp. Back on solid ground, walk a few steps south to snap a classic picture of the **Brandenburg Gate** (p26), then get lost in the haunting maze of the **Holocaust Memorial** (p28). Ponder the source of such evil on the site of **Hitler's bunker** (p32) before strolling over to **Galeries Lafayette** (p39) and the Friedrich-stadtpassagen for some retail therapy, followed by lunch at **Augustiner am Gendarmenmarkt** (p35).

☀ Grab a sweet chocolate treat at **Rausch Schokoladenhaus** (p38), take in the architectural harmony of **Gendarmenmarkt** (p32) and then follow Friedrichstrasse to Unter den Linden and continue north to the **Tränenpalast** (p32) to glean insight into the human toll the Berlin Wall took on residents on both sides.

☾ To compensate for the meaty lunch at Augustiner, enjoy a gourmet vegetarian dinner at **Cookies Cream** (p36), then grab a beer at **Berliner Republik** (p37) before wrapping up the night with cocktails at chic **Bar Tausend** (p37).

◉ Top Sights

Reichstag & Government Quarter (p24)

Brandenburg Gate (p26)

Holocaust Memorial (p28)

♥ Best of Berlin

Eating

Augustiner am Gendarmenmarkt (p35)

Cookies Cream (p36)

Shopping

Rausch Schokoladenhaus (p38)

Galeries Lafayette (p39)

Historical Sites

Reichstag (p24)

Brandenburg Gate (p26)

Tränenpalast (p32)

Getting There

🚌 **Bus** The 100, 200 and TXL run along most of Unter den Linden.

Ⓢ **S-Bahn** The S1 and S2/25 stop at Brandenburger Tor and at Friedrichstrasse.

Ⓤ **U-Bahn** The U6 runs along Friedrichstrasse with a stop near Gendarmenmarkt (Französische Strasse).

Top Sights
Reichstag & Government Quarter

The nexus of German political power snuggles neatly into the Spreebogen, a horseshoe-shaped bend in the Spree River. The historic anchor of the federal government quarter is the glass-domed Reichstag, which once rubbed against the western side of the Berlin Wall. It now forms part of the Band des Bundes (Ribbon of Federal Buildings), a series of glass-and-concrete buildings that symbolically link the former East and West Berlin across the Spree. North of the river looms the solar-panelled Hauptbahnhof (central train station).

👁 Map p30, C2

www.bundestag.de

Platz der Republik 1, Visitors' Service, Scheidemannstrasse

🕐 Visitors' Service 8am-8pm Apr-Oct, to 6pm Nov-Mar

🚌 100, **S** Brandenburger Tor, Hauptbahnhof, **U** Brandenburger Tor, Bundestag

Reichstag building

Don't Miss

Reichstag Building

The four corner towers and mighty facade with the bronze dedication 'Dem Deutschen Volke' (To the German People; added in 1916) are the only original sections of the 1894 Reichstag. Lord Norman Foster, the architectural mastermind of the building's post-reunification makeover, preserved only the historical shell and added the sparkling glass dome, Berlin's newest symbol.

Reichstag Dome

Whoever said the best things in life are free might have been thinking of the lift ride up to the rooftop of the Reichstag. Enjoy the knockout views, then pick up a free auto-activated audioguide and learn about the building, Berlin landmarks and the workings of the Bundestag while following the ramp spiralling up and around the dome's mirror-clad funnel.

Bundeskanzleramt

Germany's chancellor keeps his or her office in the H-shaped Federal Chancellery designed by Axel Schultes and Charlotte Frank. From Moltkebrücke bridge or the northern Spree River promenade you can best appreciate the circular openings that inspired the building's nickname, 'washing machine'. Eduardo Chillida's rusted-steel *Berlin* sculpture graces the forecourt.

Paul-Löbe-Haus

This vast glass-and-concrete building houses offices for the Bundestag's parliamentary committees. In a visual symbol of reunification, a double footbridge over the Spree links the building to the Marie-Elisabeth-Lüders-Haus, home to the parliamentary library.

☑ Top Tips

▶ Tickets for visiting the Reichstag dome must be prebooked online at www.bundestag.de.

▶ With any luck, you can pick up leftover tickets for the same or next day at the Reichstag Service Centre near the main entrance. Bring ID.

▶ Free multilingual audioguides are available on the roof terrace.

✗ Take a Break

Book at least two weeks ahead for a table at the **Dachgartenrestaurant Käfer** (☏030-2262 9933; www.feinkost-kaefer.de/berlin; mains €19.50-36; ☺9am-4.30pm & 6.30pm-midnight) on the Reichstag rooftop.

For snacks and beer, report to the self-service **Berlin Pavillon** (☏030-2065 4737; www.berlin-pavillon.de; Scheidemannstrasse 1; mains €3.50-9; ☺8am-9pm) on the edge of Tiergarten park.

Top Sights
Brandenburg Gate

A symbol of division during the Cold War, the landmark Brandenburg Gate (Brandenburger Tor) now epitomises German reunification and often serves as a photogenic backdrop for festivals, mega-concerts and New Year's Eve parties. It was in Athens' Acropolis that Carl Gotthard Langhans found inspiration for the elegant triumphal arch, completed in 1791 as the royal city gate.

👁 Map p30, D3

Pariser Platz

S Brandenburger Tor,
U Brandenburger Tor

Don't Miss

Quadriga

Crowning the Brandenburg Gate is Johann Gottfried Schadow's sculpture of the winged goddess of victory piloting a chariot drawn by four horses. After trouncing Prussia in 1806, Napoleon kidnapped and held her hostage in Paris until she was freed by a gallant Prussian general in 1815.

Pariser Platz

Lorded over by the gate, this elegant square was completely flattened in WWII, then spent the Cold War trapped east of the Berlin Wall. Look around now: the US, French and British embassies, banks and a luxury hotel have returned to their original sites and once again frame the bustling plaza, just as they did during its 19th century heyday.

Hotel Adlon

A near-replica of the 1907 original, the Adlon is Berlin's poshest hotel. It reportedly inspired the 1932 movie *Grand Hotel*. Now called the Adlon Kempinski, it's still a favourite haunt of the famous, powerful and eccentric. Remember Michael Jackson dangling his baby out the window? It happened at the Adlon.

The Gate

Get the gist of Berlin's often turbulent history in 20 minutes without opening a book in this new whirlwind **multimedia show** (☎030-236 078 436; www.thegate-berlin.de; Pariser Platz 4a; adult/concession/child €12/9/6; ⏰10am-8pm). Using sound effects along with historical footage and documents projected onto 87 screens arranged in a U-shape, this digital-age time capsule ticks off all the major milestones – revolutions, war, Hitler, Kennedy, the Berlin Wall, reunification – in an often emotional but historically accurate format.

☑ Top Tips

▶ Pick up maps and information at the tourist office in the gate's south wing.

▶ The gate is at its most photogenic early in the morning and at sunset.

▶ If you need a moment of peace and quiet, visit the Raum der Stille (Room of Silence) in the gate's northern wing.

▶ Check out exhibits, readings or lectures at the Academy of Arts (founded in 1696) in the glass-fronted building at Pariser Platz 4.

✖ Take a Break

If you're in need of a quick refreshment, there's a small coffee bar in the lobby of The Gate multimedia show.

Top Sights
Holocaust Memorial

It took 17 years of discussion, planning and construction, but on 10 May 2005 the Memorial to the Murdered Jews of Europe was officially dedicated. Colloquially known as the Holocaust Memorial, it's Germany's central memorial to the Nazi-planned genocide of the Third Reich. In a space the size of a football field, New York architect Peter Eisenman created 2711 sarcophagi-like stelae rising in sombre silence from undulating ground. You're free to access this labyrinth at any point and make your individual journey through it.

◉ Map p30, D4

☏ 030-2639 4336

www.stiftung-denkmal.de

Cora-Berliner-Strasse 1

🕑 field 24hr, information centre 10am-8pm Tue-Sun Apr-Sep, to 7pm Oct-Mar

Ⓢ Brandenburger Tor,
Ⓤ Brandenburger Tor

Don't Miss

Field of Stelae

At first, Peter Eisenman's massive grid of concrete columns of equal size at various heights may seem austere and unemotional, but take time to feel the coolness of the stone and contemplate the interplay of light and shadow. Then plunge into this maze of narrow passageways and give yourself over to a metaphorical sense of disorientation, confusion and claustrophobia.

Ort der Information

If the memorial itself feels rather abstract, the information centre movingly lifts the veil of anonymity from the six million Holocaust victims. A graphic timeline of Jewish persecution during the Third Reich is followed by a series of rooms documenting the fates of individuals and families. Poignant and heart-wrenching, these exhibits will leave no one untouched.

Room of Names

In this darkened and most visceral room in the information centre, the names and years of birth and death of Jewish victims are projected onto all four walls while a solemn voice reads their short biographies. It takes almost seven years to commemorate all known victims in this fashion.

Homosexuellen-Denkmal

The Gay Memorial trains the spotlight on the tremendous persecution and suffering of Europe's gay community under the Nazis. Across from the Holocaust Memorial, on the edge of Tiergarten park, it's a freestanding 4m-high off-kilter concrete cube designed by Danish-Norwegian artists (and Berlin residents) Michael Elmgreen and Ingar Dragset. A looped video plays through a warped, narrow window.

☑ Top Tips

▶ Free guided tours run at 3pm on Saturday in English and at 3pm on Sunday in German.

▶ The memorial is at its moodiest (and most photogenic) when shadows are long, ie early morning or late in the day.

▶ Last admission to the information centre is 45 minutes before closing.

▶ Audioguides cost €4 (concession €2).

✗ Take a Break

For vegan and vegetarian in a modern setting, head to **Samadhi** (☎030-2248 8850; www.samadhi-vegetarian.de; Wilhelmstrasse 77; mains €9-15; ◷noon-11pm; 🛜🖉; 🚌200).

For a wide selection of eating and drinking options, take the short stroll south to Potsdamer Platz (p60).

A   B   C   D

1

Alt-Moabit

Rahel-Hirsch-Str

Kapelleufer

Spree River

Moltkebrücke

Willy-Brandt-Str

Spreebogenpark

Karlplatz

Otto-von-Bismarck-Allee

2

Bundeskanzleramt

Bundestag
Ⓤ

Paul-Löbe-Haus

Marie-Elisabeth-Lüders-Haus

Luisenstr

Paul-Löbe-Allee

9 ◉ Haus der
Kulturen
der Welt

20 ✪

Heinrich-Von-Gagern-Str

Platz der
Republik

Reichstag
◉ ⓘ

3

John-Foster-Dulles-Allee

Yitzhak-Rabin-Str

Scheidemannstr

Ebertstr

Platz des
18 März ◉

Pariser
Platz
Ⓤ Ⓢ

Brandenburger Tor
◉ ⓘ

**Brandenburger
Tor**

Strasse des 17 Juni

Berlin Tourist Info -
Brandenburger Tor

4

Bellevueallee

Tiergartentunnel

Tiergarten

**Holocaust
Memorial** ◉

Cora-Berliner-Str

Hannah-Arendt-Str

Hitler's
Bunker 4 ◉

In den
Ministergärten

Gertrud-Kolmar-Str

Kemperplatz

Lennéstr

Am Park

Ben-Gurion-Str

Bellevuestr

Ebertstr

Vossstr

Leipziger
Platz

5

For reviews see

E

Schumannstr

Reinhardtstr

Albrechtstr

Marienstr

Bertolt-
Brecht-
Platz

18

17 9

Tränenpalast
3

Schiffbauerdamm

Reichstagufer

Bahnhof
Friedrichstr

Dorotheenstr

12 Mittelstr

25

15
14

21

Behrenstr

F

Ziegelstr

Spree River

Am Weidendamm

Plannckstr

Friedrichstr

Friedrichstr

Charlottenstr

Unter den Linden

Deutsche Bank
KunstHalle

Behrenstr

G

Johannisstr

Tucholskystr

24

Geschwister-Scholl-Str

Am Kupfergraben

Georgenstr

Bauhofstr

Am Zeughaus

Am Festungsgraben

Universitätsstr

5

6
Bebelplatz

Monbijoustr

H

Monbijou
Park
Monbijouplatz

1

**MUSEUM ISLAND
(MUSEUMSINSEL)**

Spreekanal

Bodestr

2

*Deutsches
Historisches
Museum*

2

7
*Neue
Wache*

Oberwallstr

Schlossbrücke

3

*Madame
Tussauds*

8

Französische
Str

Behrenstr

Mauerstr

Glinkastr

Jägerstr

Taubenstr

Wilhelmstr

Stadtmitte

Mohrenstr

Stadtmitte
23

Leipziger Str

Friedrichstr

10

19

11

22

Kronenstr

0
0

Französische Str

Jägerstr

16

1
Gendarmenmarkt

Taubenstr   Hausvogteiplatz

Hausvogteiplatz

Mohrenstr

Markgrafenstr

Kurstr

4

Jerusalemer Str

Niederwallstr

13

5

400 m
0.2 miles

Sights

Gendarmenmarkt   SQUARE

1 ⊙ Map p30, G4

The Gendarmenmarkt area is Berlin at its ritziest, dappled with luxury hotels, fancy restaurants and bars. The graceful square is bookended by the domed 18th-century German and French cathedrals and punctuated by a grandly porticoed concert hall, the Konzerthaus. It was named for the Gens d'Armes, an 18th-century Prussian regiment consisting of French Huguenot refugees whose story is chronicled in a museum inside the French cathedral. Climb the tower here for grand views of historic Berlin. (Ⓤ Französische Strasse, Stadtmitte)

Deutsches Historisches Museum   MUSEUM

2 ⊙ Map p30, H3

If you're wondering what the Germans have been up to for the past two millennia, take a spin around this engaging museum in the baroque Zeughaus, formerly the Prussian arsenal and now home of the German Historical Museum. Upstairs, displays concentrate on the period from the 1st century AD to the end of WWI in 1918, while the ground floor tracks the 20th century all the way through to German reunification. (German Historical Museum; ☏ 030-203 040; www.dhm.de; Unter den Linden 2; adult/concession/under

18 €8/4/free; ⊙ 10am-6pm; ☐ 100, 200, Ⓤ Hausvogteiplatz, Ⓢ Hackescher Markt)

Tränenpalast   MUSEUM

3 ⊙ Map p30, F2

During the Cold War, tears flowed copiously in this glass-and-steel border-crossing pavilion where East Berliners had to bid adieu to family visiting from West Germany – hence its moniker 'Palace of Tears'. The exhibit uses original objects (including the claustrophobic passport control booths and a border auto-firing system), photographs and historical footage to document the division's social impact on the daily lives of Germans on both sides of the border. (☏ 030-4677 7790; www.hdg.de; Reichstagufer 17; admission free; ⊙ 9am-7pm Tue-Fri, 10am-6pm Sat & Sun; Ⓢ Friedrichstrasse, Ⓤ Friedrichstrasse)

Hitler's Bunker   HISTORIC SITE

4 ⊙ Map p30, D4

Berlin was burning and Soviet tanks advancing relentlessly when Adolf Hitler killed himself on 30 April 1945, alongside Eva Braun, his long-time female companion, hours after their marriage. Today, a parking lot covers the site, revealing its dark history only via an information panel with a diagram of the vast bunker network, construction data and the site's post-WWII history. (cnr In den Ministergärten & Gertrud-Kolmar-Strasse; ⊙ 24hr; Ⓢ Brandenburger Tor, Ⓤ Brandenburger Tor)

JEAN-PIERRE LESCOURRET/GETTY IMAGES ©

Konzerthaus on Gendarmenmarkt

Deutsche Bank KunstHalle

GALLERY

5 ⦿ Map p30, G3

This small exhibition hall by American architect Richard Gluckman is a platform for contemporary art, especially from emerging art centres in Africa, China, India and South America. The three to four exhibits per year (also in cooperation with international guest curators) often push artistic boundaries and examine the effects of a globalised society. One exhibit presents Deutsche Bank's 'Artist of the Year'. (☏030-202 0930; www.deutsche-bank-kunsthalle.de; Unter den Linden 13-15; adult/concession/under 18 €4/3/free, Mon free; ☺10am-8pm; ☒100, 200, TXL, Ⓤ Französische Strasse)

Bebelplatz

SQUARE

6 ⦿ Map p30, G3

In 1933 the Nazi German Student League organised the first full-blown public book burning in Germany. Works by Brecht, Mann, Marx and others deemed 'subversive' went up in flames on this treeless square. Named for August Bebel, the co-founder of Germany's Social Democratic Party (SPD), it was originally laid out in the 18th century under King Frederick the Great. (☒100, 200, TXL, Ⓤ Hausvogteiplatz)

Understand
Berlin under the Swastika

- -

The rise to power of Adolf Hitler and the NSDAP (Nazi Party) in January 1933 had instant and far-reaching consequences for all of Germany. Within three months, all non-Nazi parties, organisations and labour unions had been outlawed and many political opponents, intellectuals and artists detained without trial. Jews, of course, were a main target from the start but the horror escalated for them during the Kristallnacht pogroms on 9 November 1938, when Nazi thugs desecrated, burned and demolished synagogues and Jewish cemeteries, property and businesses across the country. Jews had begun to emigrate after 1933, but this event set off a stampede.

The fate of those Jews who stayed behind is well known: the systematic, bureaucratic and meticulously documented annihilation in death camps, mostly in Nazi-occupied territories in Eastern Europe. Sinti and Roma (gypsies), political opponents, priests, gays and habitual criminals were targeted as well. Of the roughly seven million people who were sent to concentration camps, only 500,000 survived.

The Battle of Berlin
With the Normandy invasion of June 1944, Allied troops arrived in formidable force on the European mainland, supported by unrelenting air raids on Berlin and most other German cities. The final Battle of Berlin began in mid-April 1945, with 1.5 million Soviet troops barrelling towards the city from the east. On 30 April, when the fighting reached the government quarter, Hitler and his long-time companion Eva Braun killed themselves in their bunker. As their bodies were burning, Red Army soldiers raised the Soviet flag above the Reichstag.

Defeat & Aftermath
The Battle of Berlin ended on 2 May, with Germany's unconditional surrender six days later. The fighting had taken an enormous toll on Berlin and its people. Much of the city lay in smouldering rubble and at least 125,000 Berliners had lost their lives. In July 1945, the leaders of the Allies met in Potsdam to carve up Germany and Berlin into four zones of occupation controlled by Britain, the USA, the USSR and France.

Neue Wache
MEMORIAL

7 Map p30, H3

This columned, temple-like neoclassical structure (1818) was Karl Friedrich Schinkel's first important Berlin commission. Originally a memorial to the victims of anti-Napoleonic wars, it is now Germany's Central Memorial for the Victims of War and Dictatorship. Its austere interior is dominated by Käthe Kollwitz' heart-wrenching sculpture of a mother cradling her dead soldier son. (New Guardhouse; Unter den Linden 4; admission free; ⊙10am-6pm; 🚌100, 200, TXL)

Madame Tussauds
MUSEUM

8 Map p30, F3

No celebrity in town to snare your stare? Don't fret: at this legendary wax museum the world's biggest pop stars, Hollywood legends, sports heroes and historical icons stand still – very still – for you to snap their picture. Sure, it's an expensive haven of kitsch and camp, but where else can you have a candlelit dinner with George Clooney, play piano with Beethoven or visit the land of Azeroth from the movie *Warcraft*? Avoid wait times and save money by buying tickets online. (☎01806-545 800; www.madametussauds. com/berlin; Unter den Linden 74; adult/child €23.50/18.50; ⊙10am-7pm Sep-Jul, 9.30am-7.30pm Aug, last entry 1hr before closing; 🚌100, Ⓢ Brandenburger Tor, Ⓤ Brandenburger Tor)

Haus der Kulturen der Welt
NOTABLE BUILDING

9 Map p30, A2

This highly respected cultural centre showcases contemporary non-European art, music, dance, literature, films and theatre, and also serves as a discussion forum on zeitgeist-reflecting issues. The gravity-defying parabolic roof of Hugh Stubbins' extravagant building, designed as the American contribution to a 1957 architectural exhibition, is echoed by Henry Moore's sculpture *Butterfly* in the reflecting pool. (House of World Cultures; ☎030-3978 7175; www.hkw.de; John-Foster-Dulles-Allee 10; ⊙exhibits 11am-7pm Wed-Mon; Ⓟ; 🚌100, Ⓢ Ⅱ lauptbahnhof, Ⓤ Bundestag, Hauptbahnhof)

Eating

Augustiner am Gendarmenmarkt
GERMAN €€

10 Map p30, G4

Tourists, concert-goers and hearty-food lovers rub shoulders at rustic tables in this authentic Bavarian beer hall. Soak up the down-to-earth vibe right along with a mug of full-bodied Augustiner brew. Sausages, roast pork and pretzels provide rib-sticking sustenance, but there's also plenty of lighter (even meat-free) fare as well as good-value lunch specials. (☎030-2045 4020; www.augustiner-braeu-berlin. de; Charlottenstrasse 55; mains €6.50-26.50; ⊙10am-2am; Ⓤ Französische Strasse)

Cha Chā

THAI €€

11 Map p30, F5

Feeling worn out from sightseeing or power-shopping? No problem: a helping of massaman beef curry should quickly return you to top form for, according to the menu of this Thai nosh spot, the dish has an 'activating' effect. In fact, all menu items are described as having a 'positive eating' benefit, be it vitalising, soothing or stimulating. (030-206 259 613; www.eatchacha.com; Friedrichstrasse 63; mains €8-11; 11.30am-10pm Mon-Fri, noon-10pm Sat, 12.30-9pm Sun; S Stadtmitte)

Ishin

JAPANESE €€

12 Map p30, F3

The ambience is a bit ho-hum but who cares if the sushi is super-fresh, the rice bowls generously topped with fish or meat, and the green tea free and bottomless. Prices drop a bit during happy hour (all day Wednesday and Saturday, and until 4pm on other days). (030-2067 4829; www.ishin.de; Mittelstrasse 24; sushi platter €8.50-21, bowl €5.80-7.60; 11.30am-10pm Mon-Fri, noon-10pm Sat; S Friedrichstrasse, U Friedrichstrasse)

Goodtime

THAI €€

13 Map p30, H4

Sweep on down to this busy dining room with a garden courtyard for fragrant Thai and Indonesian dishes. Creamy curries, succulent shrimp, roast duck or an entire *rijstafel* spread (an elaborate buffet-style meal) all taste flavourful and fresh, if a bit easy on the heat to accommodate German stomachs. (030-2007 4870; www.goodtime-berlin.de; Hausvogteiplatz 11; mains €11-23.50; noon-midnight; U Hausvogteiplatz)

Crackers

INTERNATIONAL €€€

14 Map p30, F3

With Crackers, Berlin nightlife impresario Heinz 'Cookie' Gindullis transformed his former club Cookies into a cosmopolitan gastro-cathedral with an appropriately lofty ceiling. The kitchen is helmed by Stephan Hentschel who treats patrons to a menu featuring such tasties as slow-cooked rack of veal or sea bass ceviche. On weekends, DJs heat up the vibe. (030-680 730 488; www.crackersberlin.com; Friedrichstrasse 158; mains €16-36; 7pm-1am; 100, 200, TXL, U Französische Strasse)

Cookies Cream

VEGETARIAN €€€

15 Map p30, F3

Kudos if you can locate this chic herbivore haven right away. Hint: it's upstairs past a giant chandelier in the service alley of the Westin Grand Hotel. Ring the bell to enter an elegantly industrial loft for flesh-free, flavour-packed dishes from current-harvest ingredients. (030-2749 2940; www.cookiescream.com; Behrenstrasse 55; mains €25, 3-course menu €44; 6.30pm-1am Tue-Sat; U Französische Strasse)

Drinking

Lost in Grub Street
BAR

16 Map p30, H4

This cocktail bar packs a punch, so to speak. The focus here is on 'Big Bowls': huge stainless steel vessels filled with potent punch for classy and convivial sharing for two to 12 people. If that's not your thing, opt for a 'short drink', creative cocktails made from such unusual cocktail ingredients as chocolate, carrot or jalapeños. Reservation recommended. (📞030-2060 3780; www.lostingrubstreet.de; Jägerstrasse 34; ⏰7pm-late Tue-Sat; Ⓤ Hausvogteiplatz)

Bar Tausend
BAR

17 Map p30, E2

No sign, no light, no bell, just an anonymous steel door tucked under a railway bridge leads to one of Berlin's chicest bars. Behind it, flirty frocks sip raspberry mojitos alongside London Mule–cradling three-day stubbles. The eye-catching decor in the tunnel-shaped space channels '80s glam while DJs and bands fuel the vibe. The restaurant in back serves Asian-German cuisine. (📞030-2758 2070; www.tausendberlin.com; Schiffbauerdamm 11; ⏰7.30pm-late Tue-Sat; Ⓢ Friedrichstrasse, Ⓤ Friedrichstrasse)

Berliner Republik
PUB

18 Map p30, F2

Just as in a mini stock exchange, the price of beer (18 varieties on tap!) fluctuates with demand after 5pm at this tourist-friendly riverside pub. Everyone goes Pavlovian when a heavy brass bell rings, signalling rock-bottom prices. In summer, seats on the terrace are the most coveted. A full menu of home-style Berlin and

---

Understand
The Reichstag in History

Germany's federal parliament building has witnessed many milestones in the country's history. After WWI, Philipp Scheidemann proclaimed the German Republic from one of its windows. The Reichstag fire in February 1933 allowed Adolf Hitler to blame the communists and helped catapult him to power. A dozen years later, victorious Red Army troops raised the Soviet flag on the bombed-out building, which stood damaged and empty on the western side of the Berlin Wall throughout the Cold War. In the 1980s, megastars such as David Bowie, Pink Floyd and Michael Jackson performed concerts in front of the building. After the collapse of the Berlin Wall, reunification was enacted in the Reichstag in 1990. Five years later, it made headlines again when the artist couple Christo and Jeanne-Claude wrapped it in fabric. Lord Norman Foster began renovations shortly after.

German fare provides sustenance.
(☎030-3087 2293; www.die-berliner-repub-lik.de; Schiffbauerdamm 8; ⏰10am-6am; 🛜;
Ⓢ Friedrichstrasse, ⓊFriedrichstrasse)

Entertainment

Konzerthaus Berlin CLASSICAL MUSIC

19 ⭐ Map p30, G4

This top-ranked concert hall – a
Schinkel design from 1821 – counts
the Konzerthausorchester Berlin as its
'house band', but also hosts inter-national soloists, thematic concert
cycles, children's events and concerts
by the Rundfunk-Sinfonieorchester
Berlin. (☎tickets 030-203 092 101; www.
konzerthaus.de; Gendarmenmarkt 2; tickets
€15-79; ⓊStadtmitte, Französische Strasse)

Tipi am Kanzleramt CABARET

20 ⭐ Map p30, A2

Tipi stages a year-round program of
high-calibre cabaret, dance, acrobat-

Top Tip

Free Concerts

The gifted students at Berlin's
top-rated classical music academy,
the **Hochschule für Musik Hanns
Eisler** (☎tickets 030-203 092 101;
www.hfm-berlin.de; Charlottenstrasse
55; ⓊStadtmitte, Französische Strasse),
showcase their talents in several
recitals weekly, most of them free
or low-cost. They're either held on
the main campus or nearby in the
Neuer Marstall at Schlossplatz 7.

---

ics, musical comedy and magic shows
starring German and international
artists. It's all staged in a huge and
festively decorated permanent tent
stationed between the Federal Chan-cellery and the House of World Cul-tures on the edge of Tiergarten park.
Pre-show dinner is available. (☎tickets
030-3906 6550; www.tipi-am-kanzleramt.
de; Grosse Querallee; tickets €30-50; 🚌100,
Ⓢ Hauptbahnhof, ⓊBundestag)

Komische Oper OPERA

21 ⭐ Map p30, F3

Opera, operetta, musicals, ballet and
concerts from many periods are the
bread and butter of this high-profile
theatre with its tiered neo-baroque au-ditorium. Seats feature an ingenious
subtitling system that gives you the
option of reading along in German
or English. Tickets can be purchased
online or at the box office at Unter
den Linden 41. (Comic Opera; ☎tickets
030-4799 7400; www.komische-oper-berlin.
de; Behrenstrasse 55-57; tickets €10-159;
⏰box office 11am-7pm Mon-Sat, 1-4pm Sun;
🚌100, 200, TXL, ⓊFranzösische Strasse)

Shopping

Rausch Schokoladenhaus CHOCOLATE

22 🔒 Map p30, G5

If the Aztecs thought of chocolate as
the elixir of the gods, then this empo-rium of truffles and pralines must be
heaven. Bonus: the chocolate volcano
and giant replicas of Berlin landmarks

like the Brandenburg Gate or the TV Tower. The upstairs cafe-restaurant has views of Gendarmenmarkt and serves sinful drinking chocolates and cakes as well as dishes prepared and seasoned with cocoa. (📞0800 030 1918; www.rausch.de; Charlottenstrasse 60; 🕑10am-8pm Mon-Sat, 11am-8pm Sun; Ⓤ Stadtmitte)

Frau Tonis Parfum

PERFUME

23 🔒 Map p30, F5

Follow your nose to this scent-sational made-in-Berlin perfume boutique and pick up a custom blend to match your type – classic, extravagant or modern. Bestsellers include the sprightly 'Berlin Summer' with hints of mint and lemon balm. (📞030-2021 5310; www.frau-tonis-parfum.com; Zimmerstrasse 13; 🕑10am-6pm Mon-Sat; Ⓤ Kochstrasse)

Dussmann – Das Kulturkaufhaus

BOOKS, MUSIC

24 🔒 Map p30, F3

It's easy to lose track of time in this cultural playground with wall-to-wall books (with an extensive English section), DVDs and CDs, leaving no genre unaccounted for. Bonus points for the free reading-glass rentals, downstairs cafe and performance space used for concerts, political discussions and high-profile book

readings and signings. (📞030-2025 1111; www.kulturkaufhaus.de; Friedrichstrasse 90; 🕑9am-midnight Mon-Fri, to 11.30pm Sat; 🛜; Ⓢ Friedrichstrasse, Ⓤ Friedrichstrasse)

Berlin Story

BOOKS

25 🔒 Map p30, F3

Never mind the souvenirs, this store's ammo is its broad selection of Berlin-related books, maps, DVDs, CDs and magazines, in English and a dozen other languages, some published in-house. A free exhibition *The Making of Berlin* tracks 800 years of city history and includes a 30-minute movie. (📞030-2045 3842; www.berlinstory.de; Unter den Linden 40; 🕑10am-7pm Mon-Sat, to 6pm Sun; 🚌100, 200, TXL, Ⓢ Friedrichstrasse, Ⓤ Friedrichstrasse, Französische Strasse)

Explore

Museum Island & Alexanderplatz

Sightseers hit the jackpot in this central and historic area, headlined by Museum Island (Museumsinsel), a Unesco-recognised cluster of five world-class repositories brimming with six millennia of art and architecture. The Berliner Dom watches serenely over it all, including the reconstruction of the Prussian-era city palace. Nearby, Germany's highest structure, the TV Tower, anchors socialist-era Alexanderplatz.

The Sights in a Day

☀ Avoid queuing for the **Per-gamonmuseum** (p42) by prebooking your ticket online, then devote at least an hour marvelling at its ancient treasures – the Ishtar Gate, the Market Gate of Miletus etc. Snap a picture of the **Berliner Dom** (p49), then head over to the **Humboldt-Box** (p49) to find out what the fuss is all about with the reconstruction of the Berlin City Palace and to enjoy a leisurely lunch with a view from the rooftop cafe.

☀ Energy restored, open your eyes about daily life under communism at the **DDR Museum** (p49), then process your impressions during a leisurely river cruise through Berlin's historic centre. In clear weather, cap your sightseeing with bird's-eye views from the top of the **TV Tower** (p49), Germany's tallest structure.

🌙 Beer o'clock! Head to **Strandbar Mitte** (p52) for a pre-dinner drink, then indulge in a traditional German meal at **Zur Letzten Instanz** (p52) or **Brauhaus Georgbräu** (p52), or try any of the restaurants in the adjacent Scheunenviertel (p81).

 Top Sights

♥ **Best of Berlin**

Getting There

🚌 **Bus** The 100, 200 and TXL link Alexanderplatz with Museum Island.

Ⓢ **S-Bahn** S5, S7/75 and S9 all converge at Alexanderplatz.

🚊 **Tram** M4, M5 and M6 connect Alexanderplatz with Hackescher Markt.

Ⓤ **U-Bahn** U2, U5 and U8 stop at Alexanderplatz. Friedrichstrasse is the closest station to Museum Island.

Top Sights
Pergamonmuseum

Even while undergoing partial renovation, the Pergamonmuseum opens a fascinating window onto the ancient world. The palatial three-wing complex presents a rich feast of classical sculpture and monumental architecture from Greece, Rome, Babylon and the Middle East in three collections: the Collection of Antiquities, the Museum of Near Eastern Antiquities and, upstairs, the Museum of Islamic Art. Most of the pieces were excavated and spirited to Berlin by German archaeologists around the turn of the 20th century. Note that the namesake Pergamon Altar will be off limits until 2019.

◎ Map p48, A2

☎ 030-266 424 242

www.smb.museum

Bodestrasse 1-3

adult/concession €12/6

🕙10am-6pm Fri-Wed, to 8pm Thu

🚌100, 200, TXL, **S** Hackescher Markt, Friedrichstrasse

Processional Way, Ishtar Gate

Don't Miss

Market Gate of Miletus

Merchants and customers once flooded through this splendid 17m-high gate into the bustling market square of Miletus, a wealthy Roman trading town in today's Turkey. A strong earthquake levelled much of the town in the 11th century, but German archaeologists dug up the site between1903 and 1905 and managed to put the puzzle back together. The richly decorated marble gate blends Greek and Roman design features and was probably built to welcome Emperor Hadrian on his AD 126 visit to Miletus.

Orpheus Floor Mosaic

Also from Miletus hails this beautifully restored floor mosaic starring Orpheus, a gifted musician from ancient Greek mythology whose lyre playing charmed even the beasts surrounding him. It originally graced the dining room of a 2nd-century Roman villa.

Ishtar Gate

Expect your jaw to drop as you face the magnificence of this reconstructed Babylonian town gate, Processional Way and facade of the throne hall of its builder, King Nebuchadnezzar II (604–562 BC). The walls of the gate are sheathed in radiant blue and ochre glazed bricks with friezes of strutting lions, bulls and dragons representing Babylonian gods. They're so striking you can almost imagine hearing the roaring and fanfare.

Clay Tablets from Uruk

Founded in the 4th millennium BC, Uruk (in present-day Iraq) is considered one of the world's first 'mega-cities', with as many as 40,000

☑ Top Tips

▶ Avoid culture fatigue by focusing on just two of the five museums in a single day.

▶ If you do want to visit two or more museums, save money by buying the Museumsinsel ticket (€18, concession €9), good for one-day admission to all five.

▶ Arrive early or late on weekdays, or skip the queues by purchasing your ticket online.

✕ Take a Break

A short walk away, **Zwölf Apostel** (www.12-apostel. de; Georgenstrasse 2; pizza €10-15, mains €16.50-22.50) does breakfast and also has lunchtime pizza specials at heavenly prices.

inhabitants and more than 9km of city walls. Among the museum's most prized possessions are clay tablets with cuneiform scripts detailing agreements and transactions that are considered the earliest written documents known to humankind.

Stela of Hammurabi

Back in the 18th century BC, King Hammurabi of Babylon decided to assert his royal authority by having his law decrees carved into an imposing stela (upright stone slab), a copy of which anchors the Babylonian Hall. Despite their ancient pedigree, some of the phrases are still heard today, including 'an eye for an eye; a tooth for a tooth'.

Statue of Hadad

Room 2, at the far end of the Museum of Near Eastern Antiquities, showcases treasures from ancient Assyria. It is lorded over by a monumental 2800-year-old statue of a fierce-looking Hadad, the West Semitic god of storm, thunder and rain. Also note the four lion sculptures guarding the partly reconstructed inner gate of the citadel of Samal (in today's Turkey).

Caliph's Palace of Mshatta

When Ottoman sultan Abdul Hamid II wanted to get into Emperor Wilhelm II's good graces, he gave him a most generous gift: the facade of the 8th-century palace of Mshatta, in today's Jordan. A masterpiece of early Islamic art, it depicts animals and mythical

Pergamonmuseum

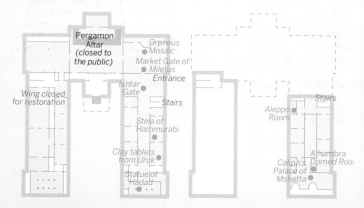

Ground Floor **Upper Floor**

Understand
Museum Island Masterplan

The Pergamonmuseum is part of Museum Island (Museumsinsel), a cluster of museums that collectively became a Unesco World Heritage Site in 1999. The distinction was at least partly achieved because of a master plan for the renovation and modernisation of the complex, which is expected to be completed in 2025 under the aegis of British architect David Chipperfield. Except for the Pergamon – now under renovation – the restoration of the buildings themselves has been completed. Construction is also well under way on the James-Simon-Galerie, a colonnaded modern foyer that will serve as the central visitor centre with ticket desks, a cafe, a shop and direct access to the Pergamonmuseum and the Neues Museum. It will also open up to the 'Archaeological Promenade', a subterranean walkway set to link to the Altes Museum and the Bode-Museum. For details see www.museumsinsel-berlin.de.

creatures frolicking peacefully amid a riot of floral motifs in an allusion to the Garden of Eden. It's upstairs in Room 9 in the Islamic Museum.

Alhambra Domed Roof

A domed cedar and poplar ceiling from the Torre de las Damas (Ladies' Tower) of the Alhambra in southern Spain's Granada forms the 'lid of the Moorish Cabinet' in the Islamic Museum. Intricately patterned, it centres on a 16-pointed star from which radiate 16 triangular panels inlaid with decorative elements.

Aleppo Room

Guests arriving in this richly painted, wood-panelled reception room would have had no doubt of the wealth and power of its owner, a Christian merchant in 17th-century Aleppo, Syria. The beautiful, if dizzying, decorations combine Islamic floral and geometric motifs with courtly scenes and Christian themes. Look closely to make out the Last Supper to the right of the central door.

Top Sights
Neues Museum

David Chipperfield's reconstruction of the bombed-out New Museum on Museum Island is the home of the show-stopping Egyptian Museum (headlined by Queen Nefertiti) and the equally enthralling Museum of Pre- and Early History. As though he was completing a giant jigsaw puzzle, the British star architect incorporated every original shard, scrap and brick he could find into the new structure, creating a brilliant blend of the historic and the modern with massive stairwells, domed rooms, muralled halls and high ceilings.

👁 Map p48, B3

📞 030-266 424 242

www.smb.museum

Bodestrasse 1-3

adult/concession €12/6

🕙10am-6pm, to 8pm Thu

🚌100, 200, TXL,
Ⓢ Hackescher Markt

Busts in Neues Museum

Don't Miss

Nefertiti
An audience with Berlin's most beautiful woman, the 3330-year-old Queen Nefertiti – she of the long graceful neck and timeless good looks – is a must. The bust was part of the treasure trove unearthed by a Berlin expedition of archaeologists around 1912 while sifting through the sands of Armana, the royal city built by Nefertiti's husband, King Akhenaten.

Berliner Goldhut
Resembling a wizard's hat, the 3000-year-old Berlin Gold Hat must indeed have struck the Bronze Age people as something magical. The entire conc is swathed in elaborate bands of astrological symbols believed to have helped priests calculate the movements of sun and moon and thus predict the best times for planting and harvesting. It's one of only four unearthed worldwide.

Berlin Grüner Kopf
A key item from the Late Egyptian Period, which shows Greek influence, is the so-called Berlin 'Green Head' (c 400 BC), the bald head of a priest carved from smooth green stone. Unusually for art from this period, the sculptor did not create a realistic portrait of a specific person but rather sought to convey universal wisdom and experience.

Trojan Collection
Three humble-looking silver jars are the star exhibits among the Trojan antiquities discovered by archaeologist Heinrich Schliemann in 1870 near Hisarlik in today's Turkey. Many other objects on display, including elaborate jewellery, ornate weapons and gold mugs, are replicas because the originals were looted by the Soviets after WWII and remain in Moscow to this day.

☑ Top Tips

▶ Skip the queue by buying your timed ticket online. Entry must be made during the designated 30-minute time slot.

▶ If you don't like crowds, visit on Thursday evening, when all exhibits on Museum Island stay open until 8pm.

▶ Make use of the excellent multilanguage audioguides included in the admission price.

✕ Take a Break

Allegretto (☎ 030 2804 2307; www.allegretto-neuesmuseum.de; Bodestrasse 1; dishes €3-10; ⏱ 10am-6pm Fri-Wed, to 8pm Thu; ☒ 100, 200, TXL, Ⓢ Hackescher Markt), the stylish cafe at the Neues Museum, serves salads, Arabic dishes and soups, plus coffee and homemade cakes.

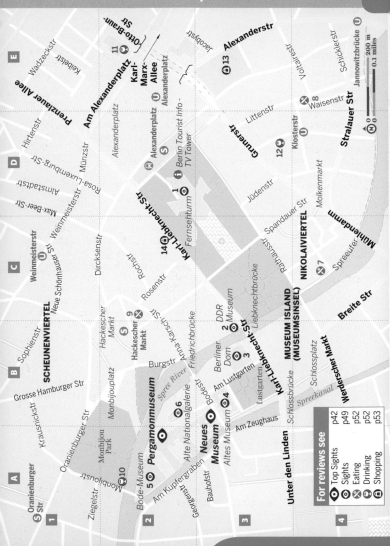

A B C D E

1
2
3
4

Wadzeckstr
Kelbelstr
Otto-Braun-Str
11
Karl-Marx-Allee
Jacobstr
Alexanderstr
13

Prenzlauer Allee
Hirtenstr
Am Alexanderplatz
Alexanderplatz
Alexanderplatz
Voltairestr
Schicklerstr
Jannowitzbrücke

Max-Beer-Str
Almstadtstr
Münzstr
Rosa-Luxemburg-Str
Neue Schönhauser Str
Alexanderplatz
Berlin Tourist Info-
TV Tower
Littenstr
Stralauer Str
Waisenstr
8
0   200 m
0   0.1 miles

Weinmeisterstr
Weinmeisterstr
Dircksenstr
Rochstr
1
Fernsehturm
Grunerstr
Klosterstr
12
9

SCHEUNENVIERTEL
Sophienstr
Krausnickstr
Hackescher
Markt
Rosenstr
Karl-Liebknecht-Str
14
Jüdenstr
Spandauer Str
Rathausstr
Molkenmarkt

Grosse Hamburger Str
Hackescher
Markt
9
Anna-Louisa-Karsch-Str
Friedrichbrücke
Liebknechtbrücke
NIKOLAIVIERTEL
7
Spreeufer
Mühlendamm

Oranienburger Str
Monbijouplatz
Burgstr
Spree River
Bodestr
Berliner
Dom
DDR
Museum
2
Breite Str

Ziegelstr
Monbijou
Park
10
Am Kupfergraben
Alte Nationalgalerie
Pergamonmuseum
6
Bode-Museum
5
Neues
Museum
4
Am Lustgarten
3
Lustgarten
Karl-Liebknecht-Str
MUSEUM ISLAND
(MUSEUMSINSEL)
Schlossplatz
Schlossbrücke
Spreekanal
Werderscher Markt

Oranienburger
Str
1
Geschwister-Scholl-Str
Bauhofstr
Altes Museum
Am Zeughaus
Unter den Linden

Karl-Marx-Allee

For reviews see

◇	Top Sights	p42
◎	Sights	p49
✕	Eating	p52
◑	Drinking	p52
◎	Shopping	p53

Sights

Fernsehturm   LANDMARK

1 ◎ Map p48, D2

Germany's tallest structure, the TV Tower has been soaring 368m high since 1969 and is as iconic to Berlin as the Eiffel Tower is to Paris. On clear days views are stunning from the panorama level at 203m or from the upstairs restaurant Sphere (mains €10 to €29), which makes one revolution per hour. To shorten the wait, buy a timed ticket online. (☎030-247 575 875; www.tv-turm.de; Panoramastrasse 1a; adult/child €13/8.50, premium ticket €19.50/12; ◷9am-midnight Mar-Oct, 10am-midnight Nov-Feb, last ascent 11.30pm; ☒100, 200, TXL, ⓤAlexanderplatz, Ⓢ Alexanderplatz)

DDR Museum   MUSEUM

2 ◎ Map p48, B3

This interactive museum does an entertaining job of pulling back the iron curtain on an extinct society. You'll learn how, under communism, kids were put through collective potty training, engineers earned little more than farmers, and everyone, it seems, went on nudist holidays. A highlight is a simulated ride in a Trabi (an East German car). (GDR Museum; ☎030-847 123 731; www.ddr-museum.de; Karl-Liebknecht-Strasse 1; adult/concession €7/5; ◷10am-8pm Sun-Fri, to 10pm Sat; ☒100, 200, TXL, Ⓢ Hackescher Markt)

Berliner Dom   CHURCH

3 ◎ Map p48, B3

Pompous yet majestic, the Italian Renaissance–style former royal court church (1905) does triple duty as house of worship, museum and concert hall. Inside it's gilt to the hilt and outfitted with a lavish marble-and-onyx altar, a 7269-pipe Sauer organ and elaborate royal sarcophagi. Climb up the 267 steps to the gallery for glorious city views. (Berlin Cathedral;

Understand

Berlin City Palace: Back to the Future

Across from Museum Island (Museumsinsel) looms Berlin's biggest construction site: the Humboldt Forum, an art and cultural centre built to look like an exact replica of the baroque Berliner Stadtschloss (Berlin City Palace), but with a modern interior. Construction finally kicked off in July 2013 after two decades of debate and bickering. The entire project should go online in 2019.

Pending the Forum's completion, the futuristic **Humboldt-Box** (☎0180 503 0707; www.humboldt-box.com; Schlossplatz 5; admission free; ◷10am-7pm Apr-Nov, to 6pm Dec-Mar; ☒100, 200, TXL, ⓤHausvogteiplatz) has interactive displays that introduce various exhibition concepts, chronicle the palace's history and explain the state-of-the-art construction technology used in its reconstruction.

☎030-2026 9136; www.berlinerdom.de; Am Lustgarten; adult/concession/under 18 €7/5/free; ⏱9am-8pm Apr-Oct, to 7pm Nov-Mar; 🚌100, 200, TXL, ⓈHackescher Markt)

242; www.smb.museum; Am Lustgarten; adult/concession €10/5; ⏱10am-6pm Tue, Wed & Fri-Sun, to 8pm Thu; 🚌100, 200, TXL, ⓈFriedrichstrasse, Hackescher Markt)

Altes Museum MUSEUM

 4 ⊙ Map p48, B3

A curtain of fluted columns gives way to the Pantheon-inspired rotunda of the grand neoclassical Old Museum, which harbours a prized antiquities collection. In the downstairs galleries, sculptures, vases, tomb reliefs and jewellery shed light on various facets of life in ancient Greece, while upstairs the focus is on the Etruscans and Romans. Top draws include the *Praying Boy* bronze sculpture, Roman silver vessels, an 'erotic cabinet' (over 18s only!) and portraits of Caesar and Cleopatra. (Old Museum; ☎030-266 424

Bode-Museum MUSEUM

 5 ⊙ Map p48, A2

On the northern tip of Museumsinsel, this palatial edifice houses a comprehensive collection of European sculpture from the early Middle Ages to the 18th century, including priceless masterpieces by Tilman Riemenschneider, Donatello and Giovanni Pisano. Other rooms harbour a precious coin collection and a smattering of Byzantine art, including sarcophagi and ivory carvings. (☎030-266 424 242; www.smb.museum; cnr Am Kupfergraben & Monbijoubrücke; adult/concession €12/6; ⏱10am-6pm Tue, Wed & Fri-Sun, to 8pm Thu; ⓈHackescher Markt, Friedrichstrasse)

 Top Tip

Sightseeing River Cruises

A lovely way to experience Berlin from April to October is from the open-air deck of a river cruiser. Several companies run relaxing Spree spins through the city centre from landing docks on the eastern side of Museumsinsel, for example outside the DDR Museum. Sip refreshments while a guide showers you with titbits (in English and German) as you glide past grand old buildings, beer gardens and the government quarter. A one-hour tour costs between €12 and €14.

Alte Nationalgalerie MUSEUM

 6 ⊙ Map p48, B2

The Greek temple-style Old National Gallery is a three-storey showcase of 19th-century European art. To get a sense of the period's virtuosity, pay special attention to the moody landscapes by Romantic heart-throb Caspar David Friedrich, the epic canvases by Franz Krüger and Adolf Menzel glorifying Prussia, the Gothic fantasies of Karl Friedrich Schinkel, and the sprinkling of French and German impressionists. (Old National Gallery; ☎030-266 424 242; www.smb.museum; Bodestrasse 1-3; adult/concession €12/6;

Understand

Red Berlin: Life in the GDR

Two Germanys

The formal division of Germany in 1949 resulted in the western zones becoming the Bundesrepublik Deutschland (BRD; Federal Republic of Germany, FRG) with Bonn as its capital, and the Soviet zone morphing into the Deutsche Demokratische Republik (DDR; German Democratic Republic, GDR) with East Berlin as its capital. Despite the latter's name, only one party – the Sozialistische Einheitspartei Deutschlands (SED; Socialist Unity Party of Germany) – controlled all policy until 1989.

The Stasi

In order to oppress any opposition, the GDR government established the Ministry for State Security (Stasi) in 1950 and put millions of its own citizens under surveillance. Tactics included wire-tapping, videotape observation and the opening of private mail. Real or suspected regime critics often ended up in Stasi-run prisons. The organisation grew steadily in power and size, and by the end had 91,000 official full-time employees plus 173,000 informants. The latter were recruited among regular folk to spy on their co-workers, friends, family and neighbours as well as on people in West Germany.

Economic Woes & the Wall

While West Germany blossomed in the 1950s, thanks to the US-sponsored Marshall Plan economic aid package, East Germany stagnated, partly because of the Soviets' continued policy of asset stripping and reparation payments. As the economic gulf widened, scores of mostly young and educated East Germans decided to seek a future in the west, further straining the economy and leading to the construction of the Berlin Wall in 1961 to stop the exodus. The appointment of Erich Honecker in 1971 opened the way for rapprochement with the west. Honecker fell in line with Soviet politics but his economic approach did improve the East German economy, eventually leading to the collapse of the regime and the fall of the Berlin Wall in November 1989.

 Local Life
Drinks with a View

There are few better places for summertime sunset cocktails than the rooftop terrace of the House of Weekend club, with the entire glittering city at your feet.

🕐10am-6pm Tue, Wed & Fri-Sun, to 8pm Thu; 🚌100, 200, TXL, Ⓢ Hackescher Markt)

Eating

Brauhaus Georgbräu GERMAN €€

 7 ✕ Map p48, C4

Long before the craft beer craze reached Berlin, this cosy brewpub already churned out its own light and dark Georg-Bräu. In winter, the woodsy beer hall is perfect for tucking into hearty Berlin-style fare, while in summer tables in the riverside beer garden are golden. (📞030-242 4244; http://brauhaus-georgbraeu.de; Spreeufer 4; mains €6-14; 🕐12pm-midnight; Ⓤ Klosterstrasse)

Zur Letzten Instanz GERMAN €€

8 ✕ Map p48, E4

Oozing folksy Old Berlin charm, this rustic eatery has been an enduring hit since 1621 and has fed everyone from Napoleon to Beethoven to Angela Merkel. Although the restaurant is now tourist-geared, the food quality is reassuringly high when it comes to such local rib-stickers as *Grillhaxe* (grilled pork knuckle) and *Bouletten* (meat patties). (📞030-242 5528; www.zurletzteninstanz.de; Waisenstrasse 14-16; mains €9-19; 🕐5pm-1am Mon, noon-1am Tue-Sat, noon-10pm Sun; Ⓤ Klosterstrasse)

Udon Kobo Ishin JAPANESE €€

 9 ✕ Map p48, C2

The simple goodness of a big, steaming bowl of chewy udon noodles (made in the open kitchen), swimming in a fragrant broth and topped with shiitakes, tofu, chicken, radishes, fish – what have you – is celebrated at this airy modern cantina-style eatery, which also serves good, value-priced sushi. (📞030-6800 4007; www.ishin.de; Litfass-Platz 1; soups €7-12; 🕐noon-2.30pm & 6-9.30pm Mon-Fri, 2-9.30pm Sat; 🚌M1, Ⓢ Hackescher Markt)

Drinking

Strandbar Mitte BAR

 10 🍷 Map p48, A2

With a full-on view of the Bode-Museum, palm trees and a relaxed ambience, Germany's first beach bar (since 2002) is great for balancing a surfeit of sightseeing stimulus with a reviving drink and thin-crust pizza. At night, there's dancing under the stars with tango, cha-cha, swing and salsa, often preceded by dance lessons. (📞030-2838 5588; www.strandbar-mitte.de; Monbijoustrasse 3; dancing €4; 🕐10am-late May-Sep; 🚌M1, Ⓢ Oranienburger Strasse)

House of Weekend　CLUB

11 Map p48, E2

In summer the House of Weekend wows with sundowners, private cabanas and 360 degree views from its sophisticated rooftop terrace. At 11pm, the 15th floor opens for hot-stepping electro with the occasional excursion into hip-hop and dubstep courtesy of top local and visiting DJs. New: six private lounges with table service behind the DJ booth. (☑reservations 0152 2429 3140; www.houseofweekend.berlin; Am Alexanderplatz 5; ☺roof garden from 7pm, weather permitting; ⑤Alexanderplatz, ⑪Alexanderplatz)

GMF　GAY

12 Map p48, D3

Berlin's premier Sunday club is known for excessive SM (standing and modelling). Currently at 2BE club. (www. gmf-berlin.de; Klosterstrasse 44; ☺11pm Sun; ⑪Klosterstrasse)

Shopping

Alexa　MALL

13 🔒 Map p48, E3

Power shoppers love this XXL mall, which cuts a rose-hued presence near Alexanderplatz. The predictable range of high-street retailers is here, plus a few more-upmarket stores like Swarovski, Crumpler, Adidas Neo and North Face. Good food court for a bite on the run. (☑030-269 3400; www.alexacentre.com; Grunerstrasse 20; ☺10am-9pm Mon-Sat; ⑤Alexanderplatz, ⑪Alexanderplatz)

ausberlin　GIFTS & SOUVENIRS

14 🔒 Map p48, C2

'Made in Berlin' is the motto of this hip shop where you can source the latest BPitch or Ostgut CD, eccentric ubo jewellery, wittily printed linen bags and all sorts of other knick-knacks (antimonster spray anyone?) designed right here in this fair city. (☑030-4199 7896; www.ausberlin.de; Karl-Liebknecht-Strasse 9; ☺10am-8pm Mon-Sat; 🛜; 🚌100, 200, TXL, ⑤Alexanderplatz, ⑪Alexanderplatz)

Explore

Potsdamer Platz

This new quarter, forged from ground once bisected by the Berlin Wall, is a showcase of fabulous contemporary architecture and home to big cinemas and shopping. Culture lovers should not skip the Kulturforum museums, especially the Gemäldegalerie, which sits right next to the world-class Berliner Philharmonie. The leafy Tiergarten, with its rambling paths, monuments and hidden beer gardens, makes for a perfect break.

RICOWDE/GETTY IMAGES ©

The Sights in a Day

Start the day getting the lay of the land by whizzing to the top of the **Panoramapunkt** (p61) for bird's-eye views of Berlin's landmarks, perhaps over a coffee. Make your way to the **Gemäldegalerie** (p56) for a rendezvous with Rembrandt and Co, then once you've exhausted your attention span, head back to Potsdamer Platz and fuel up with a light lunch at **Weilands Wellfood** (p66).

It's time to take a closer look at the futuristic architecture of the **Sony Center** (p61) before spending the afternoon delving first into the darkness of the Nazi era at the **Topographie des Terrors** (p65) and then the Cold War at **Checkpoint Charlie** (p65). By now you're probably ready for a drink, so head to **Solar** (p68) for sundown libations with a view.

Spend the evening treating your ears to a concert at the **Berliner Philharmonie** (p69) or your palate to a Michelin-starred meal at **Restaurant Tim Raue** (p66). Either way, book weeks ahead.

Top Sights

Gemäldegalerie (p56)

Potsdamer Platz (p60)

Jüdisches Museum (p62)

♥ Best of Berlin

Eating
Restaurant Tim Raue (p66)

Museums
Museum für Film und Fernsehen (p61)

Art
Gemäldegalerie (p56)

Music & Performance
Berliner Philharmonie (p69)

Getting There

🚌 **Bus** No 200 comes through en route from Bahnhof Zoologischer Garten and Alexanderplatz; M41 links the Hauptbahnhof with Kreuzberg and Neukölln via Potsdamer Platz; and the M29 connects with Checkpoint Charlie.

Ⓢ **S-Bahn** S1 and S2 link Potsdamer Platz with Unter den Linden and the Scheunenviertel.

Ⓤ **U-Bahn** U2 stops at Potsdamer Platz and Mendelssohn-Bartholdy-Park.

Top Sights
Gemäldegalerie

The Gemäldegalerie ranks among the world's finest and most comprehensive collections of European art from the 13th to the 18th centuries. Expect to feast your eyes on masterpieces by Titian, Goya, Botticelli, Holbein, Gainsborough, Canaletto, Hals, Rubens, Vermeer and many other Old Masters. The gallery's opening in a purpose-built Kulturforum space in 1998 marked the happy reunion of a collection separated by the Cold War for half a century. You're sure to find your favourites as you explore the galleries, most of them beautifully lit by muted daylight.

◉ Map p64, A2

www.smb.museum/gg

Matthäikirchplatz

adult/concession €10/5

🕐10am-6pm Tue, Wed & Fri, 10am-8pm Thu, 11am-6pm Sat & Sun

🚌M29, M48, M85, 200,
Ⓢ Potsdamer Platz,
Ⓤ Potsdamer Platz

Gemäldegalerie entrance

Don't Miss

Amor Victorius (1602–03)
Room XIV

That's quite a cheeky fellow peering down on viewers, isn't it? Wearing nothing but a mischievous grin and a pair of black angel wings, with a fistful of arrows, this Amor means business. In this famous painting, Caravaggio shows off his amazing talent at depicting objects with near-photographic realism achieved by his ingeniously theatrical use of light and shadow.

Dutch Proverbs (1559)
Room 7

In this moralistic yet humorous painting, Dutch Renaissance painter Pieter Bruegel the Elder manages to illustrate more than 100 proverbs and idioms in a single seaside village scene. While some emphasise the absurdity of human behaviour, others unmask its imprudence and sinfulness. Some sayings are still in use today, among them 'swimming against the tide' and 'armed to the teeth'.

Portrait of Hieronymus Holzschuher (1526)
Room 2

Hieronymus Holzschuher was a Nuremberg patrician, a career politician and a strong supporter of the Reformation. He was also a friend of one of the greatest German Renaissance painters, Albrecht Dürer. In this portrait, which shows its sitter at age 57, the artist brilliantly lasers in on Holzschuher's features with utmost precision, down to the furrows, wrinkles and thinning hair.

Woman with a Pearl Necklace (1662–64)
Room 18

No, it's not the *Girl with a Pearl Earring* of book and movie fame, but it's still one of Jan Vermeer's

---

☑ **Top Tips**

▶ Take advantage of the excellent free audioguide to get the low-down on selected works.

▶ Note that the room numbering system is quite confusing as both Latin (I, II, III) and Arabic (1, 2, 3) numbers are used.

▶ A tours of all 72 rooms covers almost 2km, so allow at least a couple of hours for your visit and wear comfortable shoes.

▶ Admission is free to anyone under 18.

▶ Light conditions in the gallery are best from May to September when little artificial lighting is necessary.

✕ **Take a Break**

The upstairs museum cafeteria has a salad bar, precooked meals (around €6) and hot and cold beverages.

Lunch spots on nearby Potsdamer Platz include Weilands Wellfood (p66).

most famous paintings: a young
woman studies herself in the mirror
while fastening a pearl necklace. A top
dog among Dutch Realist painters,
Vermeer mesmerises viewers by beautifully capturing this intimate moment
with characteristic soft brushstrokes.

Fountain of Youth (1546)
Room III

Lucas Cranach the Elder's poignant
painting illustrates humankind's
yearning for eternal youth. Old
crones plunge into a pool of water
and emerge as dashing hotties – this
fountain would surely put plastic sur-
geons out of business. The transition
is reflected in the landscape, which is
stark and craggy on the left, and lush
and fertile on the right.

Malle Babbe (1633)
Room 13

Frans Hals ingeniously captures the
character and vitality of his subject,
'Crazy Barbara', with free-wielding
brushstrokes. Hals met the woman
with the almost demonic laugh in the
workhouse for the mentally ill where
his son Pieter was also a resident.
The tin mug and owl are symbols of
Babbe's fondness for tipple.

Leda with the Swan (1532)
Room XV

Judging by her blissed-out expression,
Leda is having a fine time with that
swan who, according to Greek mythology, is none other than Zeus himself.
The erotically charged nature of this
painting by Italian Renaissance artist

Gemäldegalerie

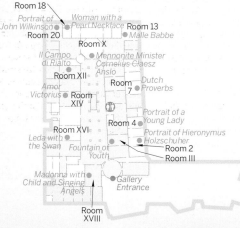

Room 18
Portrait of John Wilkinson
Room 20
Woman with a Pearl Necklace
Room 13
Malle Babbe
Room X
Il Campo di Rialto
Mennonite Minister Cornelius Claesz Anslo
Room XII
Room 7
Dutch Proverbs
Amor Victorius
Room XIV
Room 4
Portrait of a Young Lady
Room XVI
Portrait of Hieronymus Holzschuher
Leda with the Swan
Fountain of Youth
Room 2
Room III
Madonna with Child and Singing Angels
Gallery Entrance
Room XVIII

Correggio apparently so incensed its one-time owner Louis of Orléans that he cut off Leda's head with a knife. It was later restored.

Portait of a Young Lady (1470)
Room 4

Berlin's own 'Mona Lisa' may not be as famous as the real thing but she's quite intriguing nonetheless. Who is this woman with the almond-shaped eyes and porcelain skin who gazes straight at us with a blend of sadness and skepticism? This famous portrait is a key work by Petrus Christus and his only one depicting a woman.

Madonna with Child & Singing Angels (1477)
Room XVIII

Renaissance artist Sandro Botticelli's circular painting (a format called a tondo) is a symmetrical composition showing Mary at the centre flanked by two sets of four wingless angels. It's an intimate moment that shows the Virgin tenderly embracing – perhaps even about to breastfeed – her child. The white lilies are symbols of her purity.

Mennonite Minister Cornelius Claesz Anslo (1641)
Room X

A masterpiece in the gallery's prized Rembrandt collection, this large-scale canvas shows the cloth merchant and Mennonite preacher Anslo in conversation with his wife. The huge open Bible and his gesturing hand sticking out in almost 3D style from the centre of the painting are meant to emphasise the strength of his religious convictions.

Portrait of John Wilkinson (1775)
Room 20

Works by Thomas Gainsborough are rarely seen outside the UK, which is what makes this portrait of British industrialist John Wilkinson so special. Nicknamed 'Iron Mad Wilkinson' for pioneering the making and use of cast iron, here he is – somewhat ironically – shown in a natural setting, almost blending in with his surroundings.

Il Campo di Rialto (1758–63)
Room XII

Giovanni Antonio Canal, aka Canaletto, studied painting in the workshop of his theatre-set-designer father. Here he depicts the Campo di Rialto, the arcaded main market square of his hometown, Venice, with stunning precision and perspective. Note the goldsmith shops on the left, the wig-wearing merchants in the centre and the stores selling paintings and furniture on the right.

Top Sights
Potsdamer Platz

The rebirth of the historic Potsdamer Platz was
Europe's biggest building project of the 1990s. An
entire city quarter sprouted on terrain once bifurcated by the Berlin Wall that until WWII had
been the equivalent of New York's Times Square.
Today's showcase of urban renewal was masterminded by such top international architects as
Renzo Piano and Helmut Jahn and houses offices,
theatres and cinemas, hotels, apartments and
museums.

👁 Map p64, C2

Alte Potsdamer Strasse

🚌 200, ⓢ Potsdamer Platz,
ⓤ Potsdamer Platz

Aerial view of Potsdamer Platz

Don't Miss

Sony Center

Helmut Jahn's visually dramatic **Sony Center** (Potsdamer Strasse) is fronted by a 26-floor glass-and-steel tower that integrates rare relics from the pre-war Potsdamer Platz. These include a section of facade of the Hotel Esplanade and the opulent Kaisersaal hall, whose 75m move to its current location required some wizardly technology.

Museum für Film und Fernsehen

This Sony Center **museum** (☑030-300 9030; www. deutsche-kinemathek.de; Potsdamer Strasse 2; adult/concession €7/4.50, free 4-8pm Thu; ☺10am-6pm Tue, Wed & Fri-Sun, to 8pm Thu) charts milestones in German film and TV history. Most engaging are the galleries dedicated to pioneers such as Fritz Lang, ground-breaking movies such as Leni Riefenstahl's *Olympia*, German exiles in Hollywood and diva extraordinaire Marlene Dietrich.

Panoramapunkt

Europe's fastest **lift** (☑030-2593 7080; www.panorama-punkt.de; Potsdamer Platz 1; adult/concession €6.50/5, without wait €10.50/8; ☺10am-8pm Apr-Oct, to 6pm Nov-Mar) yoyos up and down the red-brick postmodern Kollhof Building. From the 100m viewing platform, a stunning 360-degree panorama reveals the city's layout. Study key moments in Potsdamer Platz history by taking in the exhibit, then relax in the cafe.

Weinhaus Huth

The 1912 Weinhaus Huth, one of the first steel-frame buildings in town, was the only Potsdamer Platz structure to survive WWII intact. The **Daimler Contemporary Berlin** (☑030-2594 1420; www.art.daimler.com; Alte Potsdamer Strasse 5, Weinhaus Huth, 4th fl; admission free; ☺11am-6pm) showcases international abstract, conceptual and minimalist art. Ring the bell to be buzzed in.

☑ **Top Tips**

▸ Check out the Berlin Wall segments outside the Potsdamer Platz S-Bahn station entrance.

▸ From September to June, free classical concerts draw music lovers to the nearby Philharmonie (p69) at 1pm on Tuesdays.

✗ **Take a Break**

For a snack with view of the Sony Center plaza from above, head to the **Helene-Schwarz-Cafe** (☑030-7202 4799; www. dffb.de; Potsdamer Strasse 2; dishes €3.50-8; ☺9am-3.30pm Mon-Fri) on the 9th floor of the Filmhaus building.

Fantastic ice cream can be had at **Caffe e Gelato** (☑030-2529 7832; www.caffe-e-gelato. de; Alte Potsdamer Strasse 7; scoops €1.70; ☺10am-10.30pm Mon-Thu, to 11pm Fri, to midnight Sat, 10.30am-10pm Sun) in the Potsdamer Platz Arkaden mall.

Top Sights
Jüdisches Museum

In a landmark building by American-Polish architect Daniel Libeskind, Berlin's Jewish Museum offers a chronicle of trials and triumphs in 2000 years of German-Jewish history. The exhibit smoothly navigates all major periods, from the Romans and the Middle Ages to the Age of Enlightenment and the community's renaissance today. Find out about Jewish cultural contributions, holiday traditions, the difficult road to emancipation and outstanding individuals and the fates of ordinary people and families.

⊙ Map p64, E4

www.jmberlin.de

Lindenstrasse 9-14

adult/concession €8/3, audioguide €3

🕐10am-8pm Tue-Sun, to 10pm Mon, last entry 1hr before closing

Ⓤ Hallesches Tor, Kochstrasse

Jüdisches Museum

Don't Miss

The Building

Libeskind's architectural masterpiece is essentially a 3D metaphor for the tortured history of the Jewish people. Its zigzag shape symbolises a broken Star of David; its silvery titanium-zinc walls are sharply angled; and instead of windows there are only small gashes piercing the building's gleaming facade.

Axes

The visual allegory continues inside, where a steep staircase descends to three intersecting walkways – called 'axes' – representing the fates of Jews during the Nazi years: death, exile and continuity. Only the latter leads to the exhibit.

Schalecket (Fallen Leaves)

Menashe Kadishman's art installation is one of the museum's most poignant. More than 10,000 open-mouthed faces cut from rusty iron plates lie scattered on the floor in an ocean of silent screams. The space itself, a soaring but claustrophobic concrete-walled enclosure that Libeskind calls a 'void', commemorates Europe's murdered Jews.

Moses Mendelssohn Exhibit

Philosopher Moses Mendelssohn (1729–86) was a key figure in the Jewish Enlightenment. His progressive thinking and lobbying paved the way for the Emancipation Edict of 1812, which made Jews full Prussian citizens with equal rights.

Max Liebermann Self-Portrait

Max Liebermann (1847–1935) was Germany's most famous impressionist, and co-founder of the Berlin Secession movement. This painting shows the Jewish artist as an old man in 1929, wearing his signature Panama hat.

☑ **Top Tips**

▶ Tickets are also valid for reduced admission on the same day and the next two days to the Berlinische Galerie (p66), a survey of 150 years of Berlin art, located just 500m away.

▶ Rent the audioguide (€3) for a more in-depth experience.

▶ Free themed tours (in German) take place at 3pm on Saturday and at 11am and 2pm on Sunday.

▶ Budget at least two hours to visit the museum, plus extra time to go through the airport-style entrance security checks.

✗ **Take a Break**

For a refuelling stop, pop by the museum's **Café Schmus** (☏030-2579 6751; www.koflerkompanie. com; dishes €5.50-8; ⊙10am-8pm Tue-Sun, to 10pm Mon) for modern takes on traditional Jewish cuisine.

WORLDWIDE/SHUTTERSTOCK ©

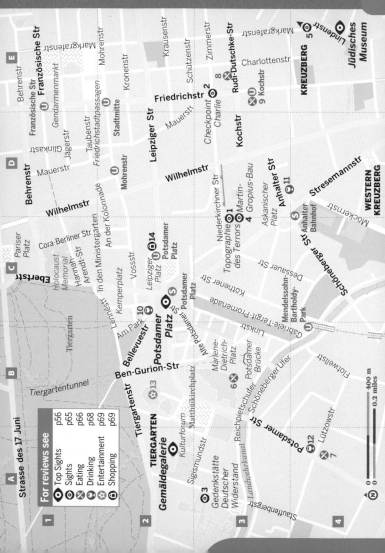

Strasse des 17 Juni

Ebertstr

Pariser Platz

Holocaust Memorial

Cora-Berliner Str

Hannah-Arendt-Str

In den Ministergärten

An der Kolonnade

Vossstr

Lennéstr

Kemperplatz

Am Park ⑩

Behrenstr

Wilhelmstr

Behrenstr

Französische Str

Markgrafenstr

Behrenstr

Mohrenstr

Glinkastr

Jägerstr

Taubenstr

Friedrichstadtpassagen

Gendarmenmarkt

Französische Str Ⓤ

Stadtmitte Ⓤ

Mauerstr

Kronenstr

Mohrenstr Ⓤ

Mauerstr

Krausenstr

Zimmerstr

Schützenstr

Leipziger Str

Friedrichstr ⓈⓊ

Checkpoint Charlie ②

Rudi-Dutschke-Str

8

9 Kochstr ⓄⓉ

Kochstr Ⓤ

Charlottenstr

Markgrafenstr

⑤ Lindenstr Ⓞ

KREUZBERG

Jüdisches Museum

Wilhelmstr

Leipziger Str Ⓤ ⑭

Potsdamer Platz Ⓤ

Niederkirchner Str

Martin-Ⓞ①

Gropius-Bau ④

Topographie des Terrors

Askanischer Platz

Anhalter Str

⑪

Stresemannstr

WESTERN KREUZBERG

Möckernstr

Ⓢ **Anhalter Bahnhof**

Dessauer Str

Schöneberger Str

Ⓤ

Gabriele-Tergit-Promenade

Mendelssohn-Bartholdy-Park

Tiergarten

Tiergartentunnel

Tiergartentunnel

Bellevuestr

Potsdamer Platz ⓈⓊ

Alte Potsdamer Str

Potsdamer Platz Str

Marlene-Dietrich-Platz

Ⓤ

⑥ ✕

Linkstr

Köthener Str

Potsdamer Brücke

Reichpietschufer

Schöneberger Ufer

Landwehrkanal

Flottwellstr

Ben-Gurion-Str

Tiergartenstr

☆ ⑬

TIERGARTEN

Gemäldegalerie

Kulturforum

Sigismundstr

Matthäikirchplatz

Gedenkstätte Deutscher Widerstand

③

⑫ ①

✕ ⑦

Lützowstr

Potsdamer Str

Stauffenbergstr

For reviews see	
◆ Top Sights	p56
◉ Sights	p65
✕ Eating	p66
⌾ Drinking	p68
★ Entertainment	p69
⊞ Shopping	p69

Ⓝ 0 ————— 400 m
0 ————— 0.2 miles

Sights

Topographie des Terrors
MUSEUM

1 Map p64, C3

In the same spot where the most feared institutions of Nazi Germany (including the Gestapo headquarters and the SS central command) once stood, this compelling exhibit chronicles the stages of terror and persecution, puts a face on the perpetrators and details the impact these brutal institutions had on all of Europe. A second exhibit outside zeroes in on how life changed for Berlin and its people after the Nazis made it their capital. (Topography of Terror; ☏030-2548 0950; www.topographie.de; Niederkirchner Strasse 8; admission free; ☺10am-8pm, grounds close at dusk or 8pm at the latest; ⑤Potsdamer Platz, ⓊPotsdamer Platz)

Checkpoint Charlie
HISTORIC SITE

2 Map p64, E3

Checkpoint Charlie was the principal gateway for foreigners and diplomats between the two Berlins from 1961 to 1990. Unfortunately, this potent symbol of the Cold War has degenerated into a tacky tourist trap, though a free open-air exhibit that illustrates milestones in Cold War History is one redeeming aspect. (cnr Zimmerstrasse & Friedrichstrasse; admission free; ☺24hr; ⓊKochstrasse)

Checkpoint Charlie

Gedenkstätte Deutscher Widerstand
MEMORIAL

3 Map p64, A3

This important exhibit on German Nazi resistance occupies the very rooms where high-ranking officers led by Claus Schenk Graf von Stauffenberg plotted the assassination attempt on Hitler on 20 July 1944. There's a memorial in the courtyard where the main conspirators were shot right after the failed coup, a story poignantly retold in the 2008 movie *Valkyrie*. (German Resistance Memorial Centre; ☏030-2699 5000; www.gdw-berlin.de; Stauffenbergstrasse 13-14, enter via courtyard; admission free; ☺9am-6pm Mon-Wed & Fri, 9am-8pm Thu, 10am-6pm

Sat & Sun; M29, M48, Ⓢ Potsdamer Platz, Ⓤ Potsdamer Platz, Kurfürstenstrasse)

Martin-Gropius-Bau
GALLERY

4 Map p64, C3

With its mosaics, terracotta reliefs and airy atrium, this Italian Renaissance–style exhibit space named for its architect (Bauhaus founder Walter Gropius' great-uncle) is a celebrated venue for high-calibre travelling shows. Whether it's a David Bowie retrospective, the latest works of Ai Weiwei or an ethnological exhibit on the mysteries of Angkor Wat, it's bound to be well curated and utterly fascinating. (☏030-254 860; www.gropiusbau.de; Niederkirchner Strasse 7; cost varies, under 16 free; ◷10am-7pm Wed-Mon; 🚌M41, Ⓢ Potsdamer Platz, Ⓤ Potsdamer Platz)

Berlinische Galerie
GALLERY

5 Map p64, E4

This gallery in a converted glass warehouse is a superb spot for taking stock of what Berlin's art scene has been up to since 1870. Temporary exhibits occupy the ground floor from where two floating stairways lead upstairs to selections from the permanent collection which is especially strong when it comes to Dada, New Objectivity, Eastern Europe avant-garde, and art created during the Cold War. (Berlin Museum of Modern Art, Photography & Architecture; ☏030-7890 2600; www.berlinischegalerie.de; Alte Jakobstrasse 124-128; adult/concession/under 18 €8/5/free; ◷10am-6pm Wed-Mon; Ⓤ Kochstrasse, Moritzplatz)

Eating

Weilands Wellfood
INTERNATIONAL €

6 Map p64, B3

The wholewheat pastas, vitamin-packed salads and fragrant wok dishes at this jazzy self-service bistro are perfect for health- and waist-watchers but don't sacrifice a thing to the taste gods. Sit outside by the little pond, ideally outside of the office lunch rush. (☏030-2589 9717; www.weilands-wellfood.de; Marlene-Dietrich-Platz 1; mains €5-10; ◷10am-8pm Mon-Fri, noon-8pm Sat & Sun; �🖊; 🚋200, Ⓢ Potsdamer Platz, Ⓤ Potsdamer Platz)

Joseph-Roth-Diele
GERMAN €

7 Map p64, A4

Named for an Austrian Jewish writer, this wood-panelled salon time-warps you back to the 1920s, when Roth used to live next door. Walls decorated with bookshelves and quotations from his works draw a literary, chatty crowd, especially at lunchtime when two daily changing €5 specials supplement the hearty menu of German classics. Pay at the counter. (☏030-2636 9884; www.joseph-roth-diele.de; Potsdamer Strasse 75; dishes €4-12; ◷10am-midnight Mon-Fri; Ⓤ Kurfürstenstrasse)

Restaurant Tim Raue
ASIAN €€€

8 Map p64, E3

Now here's a two-star Michelin restaurant we can get our mind around. Unstuffy ambience and a reduced design

Understand

The Berlin Wall

It's more than a tad ironic that one of Berlin's most popular tourist attractions is one that no longer exists. For 28 years the Berlin Wall, the most potent symbol of the Cold War, divided not only a city but the world.

The Beginning

Shortly after midnight on 13 August 1961, East German soldiers and police began rolling out miles of barbed wire that would soon be replaced with prefabricated concrete slabs. The Wall was a desperate measure launched by the German Democratic Republic (GDR) government to stop the sustained brain and brawn drain the country had experienced since its 1949 founding. Some 3.6 million people had already headed to western Germany, putting the GDR on the brink of economic and political collapse.

The Physical Border

Euphemistically called the 'Anti-Fascist Protection Barrier', the Berlin Wall was continually reinforced and refined. It eventually grew into a complex border-security system consisting of two walls enclosing a 'death strip' riddled with trenches, floodlights, attack dogs, electrified alarm fences and watchtowers staffed by guards with shoot-to-kill orders. Nearly 100,000 GDR citizens tried to escape, many using spectacular contraptions like homemade hot-air balloons or U-boats. There are no exact numbers, but it is believed that hundreds died in the process.

The End

The Wall's demise came as unexpectedly as its creation. Once again the GDR was losing its people in droves, this time via Hungary, which had opened its borders with Austria. Major demonstrations in East Berlin came to a head in early November 1989 when half a million people gathered on Alexanderplatz. Something had to give. It did on 9 November, when a GDR spokesperson mistakenly announced during a press conference on live TV that all travel restrictions to the West would be lifted immediately. Amid scenes of wild partying, the two Berlins came together again. Today, only about 2km of the hated barrier still stands, most famously the 1.3km-long East Side Gallery. In addition, a double row of cobblestones embedded in the pavement and 32 information panels guide visitors along 5.7km of the Wall's course.

with walnut and Vitra chairs perfectly juxtapose with Raue's brilliant Asian-inspired plates that each shine the spotlight on a few choice ingredients. His interpretation of Peking duck is a perennial bestseller. Popular at lunchtime too. (📞030-2593 7930; www.tim-raue.com; Rudi-Dutschke-Strasse 26; 3-/4-course lunch €48/58, 8-course dinner €198, mains €55-66; ⏰noon-3pm & 7pm-midnight Wed-Sat; Ⓤ Kochstrasse)

Nobelhart & Schmutzig INTERNATIONAL €€€

9 Map p64, E3

'Brutally local' is the motto at the Michelin-starred restaurant of star sommelier Billy Wagner. All ingredients hail – without exception – from producers in and around Berlin and the nearby Baltic Sea. Hence, no pepper or lemons. The intellectually ambitious food is fresh and seasonal or naturally preserved by using such traditional methods as pickling, brining and fermenting. (📞030-2594 0610; www.nobelhartundschmutzig.com; Friedrichstrasse 218; 10-course menu €80; ⏰6.30pm-midnight; Ⓤ Kochstrasse)

Drinking

Fragrances COCKTAIL BAR

10 Map p64, C2

Berlin cocktail maven Arnd Heissen's newest baby is the world's first 'perfume bar', a libation station where he mixes potable potions mimicking famous scents. The black-mirrored

space in the **Ritz-Carlton** (📞030-337 777; www.ritzcarlton.com; Potsdamer Platz 3; d from €190-435; Ⓟ🛎❄@🛜♿; Ⓢ Potsdamer Platz, Ⓤ Potsdamer Platz) is a like a 3D menu where adventurous drinkers sniff out their favourite from among a row of perfume bottles, then settle back into flocked couches to enjoy exotic blends served in unusual vessels, including a birdhouse. (📞030-337 777; www.ritzcarlton.com; Ritz-Carlton, Potsdamer Platz 3; ⏰from 7pm Wed-Sat; 🛜; 🍽200, Ⓢ Potsdamer Platz, Ⓤ Potsdamer Platz)

Solar BAR

11 Map p64, D3

Watch the city light up from this 17th-floor glass-walled sky lounge above a posh restaurant (mains €18 to €37). With its dim lighting, soft black leather couches and breathtaking views, it's a great spot for a date or sunset drinks. Getting there aboard an exterior glass lift is half the fun. The entrance is behind the Pit Stop auto shop. (📞0163 765 2700; www.solar-berlin.de; Stresemannstrasse 76; ⏰6pm-2am Sun-Thu, to 3am Fri & Sat; Ⓢ Anhalter Bahnhof)

Kumpelnest 3000 BAR

12 Map p64, A4

A former brothel, this trashy bat cave started out as an art project and would be kooky and kitsch enough to feature in a 1940s Shanghai noir thriller. Famous for its wild, debauched all-nighters, it attracts a hugely varied crowd, including the occasional celebrity (Kate Moss, U2,

Karl Lagerfeld). (📞030-261 6918; www.
kumpelnest3000.com; Lützowstrasse 23;
🕐7pm-5am or later; Ⓤ Kurfürstenstrasse)

Entertainment

Berliner
Philharmonie   CLASSICAL MUSIC

13 ⭐ Map p64, B2

This world-famous concert hall has
supreme acoustics and, thanks to
Hans Scharoun's terraced vineyard
configuration, not a bad seat in the
house. It's the home turf of the Berliner Philharmoniker, who will be led by
Sir Simon Rattle until 2018. One year
later, Russia-born Kirill Petrenko will
pick up the baton as music director.
(📞tickets 030-254 888 999; www.berliner-
philharmoniker.de; Herbert-von-Karajan-
Strasse 1; tickets €30-100; 🚌M29, M48, M85,
200, Ⓢ Potsdamer Platz, Ⓤ Potsdamer Platz)

Shopping

LP12 Mall of Berlin   MALL

14 🔒 Map p64, C2

This spanking new retail quarter is
tailor-made for black-belt mall rats.
More than 270 shops vie for your
shopping euros, including flagship
stores by Karl Lagerfeld, Hugo Boss,
Liebeskind, Marc Cain, Muji and
other international high-end brands
alongside the usual high-street chains
like Mango and H&M. Free mobile-
phone recharge station on the 2nd

Top Tip

Kulturforum Museums

In addition to the famous
Gemäldegalerie (p56) and **Neue
Nationalgalerie** (which is closed
for renovations), the Kulturforum
encompasses three other top-rated
museums: the **Kupferstichkabinett**
(Museum of Prints and Drawings; 📞030-
266 424 242; www.smb.museum/kk;
Matthäikirchplatz; adult/concession €6/3;
🕐10am-6pm Tue-Fri, 11am-6pm Sat &
Sun; 🚌M29, M48, M85, 200, Ⓢ Potsdamer
Platz, Ⓤ Potsdamer Platz) with prints
and drawings dating from the 14th
century; the **Musikinstrumenten-
Museum** (Musical Instruments Museum;
📞030-2548 1178; www.mim-berlin.de;
Tiergartenstrasse 1, enter via Ben-Gurion-
Strasse; adult/concession/under 18 €6/3/
free; 🕐9am-5pm Tue, Wed & Fri, 9am-8pm
Thu, 10am-5pm Sat & Sun; 🚌200, Ⓢ Potsdamer Platz, Ⓤ Potsdamer Platz) with
rare historical instruments; and the
Kunstgewerbemuseum (Museum of
Decorative Arts; 📞030-266 424 242; www.
smb.museum; Matthäikirchplatz, adult/
concession/under 18 €8/4/free; 🕐10am-
6pm Tue-Fri, 11am-6pm Sat & Sun; 🚌M29,
M48, M85, 200, Ⓢ Potsdamer Platz,
Ⓤ Potsdamer Platz), with its prized
collection of arts and crafts. 'Area
tickets' valid for one-day admission
at all costs €12.

floor. (www.mallofberlin.de; Leipziger Platz
12; 🕐10am-9pm Mon-Sat; 📶; 🚌200,
Ⓤ Potsdamer Platz, Ⓢ Potsdamer Platz)

Local Life
An Afternoon in the Bergmannkiez

Getting There

The Bergmannkiez is in the western part of Kreuzberg.

U U-Bahn To start the itinerary, get off at Gneisenaustrasse (U7). When you're finished, Mehringdamm station (U6 and U7) is closest.

One of Berlin's most charismatic neighbourhoods, the Bergmannkiez in gentrified western Kreuzberg is named for its main shopping strip, the Bergmannstrasse, which is chock-a-block with people-watching cafes and indie shops and boutiques. Nearby Tempelhof Airport saw its finest hour during the 1948–49 Berlin Blockade and is now a vast urban park. Above it all 'soars' the Kreuzberg hill, Berlin's highest natural elevation and a wonderful summertime play zone.

① Marheineke Markthalle

Thanks to a substantial renovation, the historic **Marheineke Markthalle** (www.meine-markthalle.de; Marheineke-platz; ⏰8am-8pm Mon-Fri, to 6pm Sat; Ⓤ Gneisenaustrasse) has traded its grungy 19th-century charm for bright and modern digs. Its aisles brim with vendors plying everything from organic sausages to handmade cheeses, artisanal honey and other bounty.

② Colours

Vintage fans love **Colours** (☏030-694 3348; www.kleidermarkt-vintage.de; Bergmannstrasse 102, 1st fl; ⏰11am-7pm Mon-Sat; Ⓤ Mehringdamm), a huge loft with used clothing going back to the 1960s and a smaller selection of new street and club-wear threads, all priced by the kilo. Enter via the courtyard.

③ Chamissoplatz

With its ornate townhouses, cobbled streets, old-timey lanterns and even an octagonal pissoir, **Chamissoplatz** looks virtually unchanged since the late 19th century, which is why this square is often used as a film set. Organic farmers market on Saturdays.

④ Tempelhofer Feld

Decommissioned Tempelhof Airport, which so gloriously handled the Berlin Airlift of 1948–49, has been repurposed as a vast untamed **urban park** (☏030-200 037 441; www.thf-berlin. de; enter via Oderstrasse, Tempelhofer Damm or Columbiadamm; tours adult/concession €13/9; ⏰sunrise to sunset, tours in English 1.30pm & 3.30pm Wed & Fri, 3pm Sat, 2pm Sun; Ⓤ Paradestrasse, Boddinstrasse, Leinestrasse). It's a wonderfully noncommercial, creative, open-sky space with a beer garden, art installations, urban gardening, barbecue areas and other fun zones. Enter from Columbiadamm.

⑤ Luftbrückendenkmal

The **Berlin Airlift Memorial** (Platz der Luftbrücke; Ⓢ Platz der Luftbrücke) outside the former Tempelhof Airport honours those who participated in keeping the city fed and free during the 1948–49 Berlin Blockade. The trio of spikes represents the three air corridors used by the Western Allies, while the plinth bears the names of the 79 people who died in this colossal effort.

⑥ Viktoriapark

Take a break in this rambling park draped over the 66m-high Kreuzberg hill, home to a vineyard, a waterfall and a pompous memorial commemorating Napoleon's 1815 defeat. In summer, laid-back locals arrive to chill, tan or enjoy beers at **Golgatha** (☏030-785 2453; www.golgatha-berlin.de; Dudenstrasse 48-64; ⏰9am-late Apr-Sep; Ⓢ Yorckstrasse, Ⓤ Platz der Luftbrücke).

⑦ Curry 36

Day after day, night after night, a motley crowd – cops, cabbies, queens, office jockeys, savvy tourists etc – wait their turn at **Curry 36** (☏030-2580 088 336; www.curry36.de; Mehringdamm 36; snacks €2-6; ⏰9am-5am; Ⓤ Mehringdamm), a top *Currywurst* purveyor that's been frying 'em up since 1981.

Explore

Scheunenviertel

The Scheunenviertel (Barn Quarter) is one of Berlin's oldest, most charismatic neighbourhoods. Embark on an aimless wander and you'll constantly stumble upon enchanting surprises: here an idyllic courtyard or bleeding-edge gallery, there a fashion-forward boutique or belle époque ballroom. Since reunification, the Scheunenviertel has also reprised its historic role as Berlin's main Jewish Quarter.

BUSÁ PHOTOGRAPHY/GETTY IMAGES ©

The Sights in a Day

☀ Make your way to Nordbahnhof S-Bahn station to start the day with an in-depth study of the Berlin Wall at the **Gedenkstätte Berliner Mauer** (p74). Follow Bernauer Strasse east to Brunnenstrasse, then either walk south past galleries, boutiques and cafes, or hop on the U8 for the one-stop ride to Rosenthaler Platz and lunch at **Chèn Chè** (p81).

☼ Spend the afternoon rambling around the Scheunenviertel and sourcing Berlin fashions and accessories in the **Hackesche Höfe** (p78) and along Alte Schönhauser Strasse, Neue Schönhauser Strasse, Münzstrasse, Rosenthaler Strasse and their side streets. Get your art fix at **KW Institute for Contemporary Art** (p79) and follow up with a strong cuppa in its courtyard Café Bravo. Interested in Berlin's Jewish community? Swing by the **Neue Synagoge** (p79) and **Haus Schwarzenberg** (p82).

☾ Make dinner reservations at **Katz Orange** (p82) or **Pauly Saal** (p82) for modern German fare. Grab a cocktail at **Buck and Breck** (p83), then hit the dance floor at the endearingly retro **Clärchens Ballhaus** (p83).

 Top Sights

Gedenkstätte Berliner Mauer (p74)

❤ **Best of Berlin**

Eating

Schwarzwaldstuben (p82)

Hummus & Friends (p81)

Pauly Saal (p82)

Shopping

Bonbonmacherei (p84)

Ampelmann Berlin (p85)

1. Absinth Depot Berlin (p85)

Getting There

Ⓤ **U-Bahn** Weinmeisterstrasse (U8) is the most central station. Rosenthaler Platz (U8), Rosa-Luxemburg-Platz (U2) and Oranienburger Tor (U6) are closer to Torstrasse and the northern Scheunenviertel.

Ⓢ **S-Bahn** Hackescher Markt (S5, S7 and S9) and Oranienburger Strasse (S2) stations are both good jumping-off points.

🚋 **Tram** M1 runs from Museums-insel (Museum Island) to Prenz-lauer Berg and stops throughout the Scheunenviertel.

🚌 **Bus** No 142 runs along Torstrasse.

Top Sights
Gedenkstätte Berliner Mauer

For an insightful primer on the Berlin Wall, there's no better place in town than this indoor/outdoor memorial. It explains the physical layout of the barrier and the death strip, how the border fortifications were enlarged and perfected over time and what impact they had on the daily lives of people on both sides of the Wall. Exhibits follow its original course for 1.4km along Bernauer Strasse and include an original section of the barrier, vestiges of the border installations and multimedia stations.

👁 Map p76, C1

www.berliner-mauer-gedenkstaette.de

admission free

🕑 visitor centre 10am-6pm Tue-Sun, open-air exhibit 8am-10pm daily

Ⓢ Nordbahnhof, Bernauer Strasse, Eberswalder Strasse

Graffiti at the Gedenkstätte Berliner Mauer

Don't Miss

National Monument to German Division
The central memorial consists of a 70m section of original wall bounded by two rusted steel flanks. Behind it is a reconstructed 'death strip' complete with a guard tower, a security patrol path and the lamps that bathed it in fierce light at night.

Berliner Mauer Dokumentationszentrum
This exhibit puts the barrier's construction and demise into a political context and uses artefacts, documents and videos to show how it affected daily life on both sides.

Kapelle der Versöhnung
The simple but radiant Chapel of Reconciliation stands on the spot of an 1894 brick church detonated in 1985 to make room for a widening of the border strip.

Window of Rembrance
A wall of photographic portraits gives identity to the would-be escapees who lost their lives at the Berlin Wall. The parklike area surrounding the installation was once part of the adjacent cemetery.

Nordbahnhof 'Ghost Station'
The Wall also divided the city's transportation system. Three train lines that originated in West Berlin had to travel beneath East Berlin before returning to stations on the western side. At heavily guarded 'ghost-stations', trains slowed but did not stop; S-Bahn station Nordbahnhof has an exhibit on the subject.

Tunnel 29
An exhibit highlights the world-famous Tunnel 29 which for 135m below Bernauer Strasse and allowed 29 people to escape from East Berlin in September 1962.

☑ Top Tips

▶ If you have limited time, spend it in the first section between Gartenstrasse and Ackerstrasse.

▶ Enjoy sweeping views of the memorial from the viewing tower of the Documentation Centre near Ackerstrasse.

▶ The visitor centre has free maps and screens a short introductory film.

▶ The Chapel of Reconciliation hosts a 15-minute memorial service to Wall victims at noon Tuesday to Friday.

✖ Take a Break

Head to **Ost-West Cafe** (☏ 030-4677 6016; www.ost-west-cafe.de; Brunnenstrasse 53; mains €4.50-7; ⊙ 8am-10pm; 🛜) for simple international dishes amid Cold War–era themed decor.

Arty **Jää Äär** (www.facebook.com/jaaaar berlin; Brunnenstrasse 56; ⊙ 10am-10pm Wed, Sat & Sun, to 8pm Tue, Thu & Fri; 🛜) has excellent coffee, Estonian beer and homemade sandwiches.

A   B   C   D

Streltzer Str

For reviews see
◉	Top Sights	p74
◉	Sights	p78
✖	Eating	p81
🍷	Drinking	p83
✪	Entertainment	p84
🔒	Shopping	p84

Bernauer Str

◉ **Gedenkstätte Berliner Mauer**

Bergstr

Ackerstr

Ⓢ **Nordbahnhof**

Chausseestr

Habersaathstr

Gartenstr

Bergstr

Invalidenstr

✖12

Naturkundemuseum ⒰ ◉16

Eichendorffstr

Museum für Naturkunde ◉4

Schlegelstr

Tieckstr

Gartenstr

◉2 **Invalidenstr**

Chausseestr

Novalisstr

Hannoversche Str

✖11

Torstr

KW Institute for Contemporary Art

Luisenstr

Hessische Str

Linienstr

6◉

Oranienburger Tor ⒰

Oranienburger Str

Auguststr

✖13

Heckmannstr Höfe

Oranienburger Str Ⓢ

🔒20

◉5 8

7✖

Johannisstr

Neue Synagoge ✖

Friedrichstr

Kalkscheunenstr

Tucholskystr

Monbijoustr

Sammlung Boros ◉3

Schumannstr

Albrechtstr

Reinhardtstr

✪19

Ziegelstr

Sights

Hackesche Höfe
HISTORIC SITE

1 Map p76, F5

The Hackesche Höfe is the largest and most famous of the courtyard ensembles peppered throughout the Scheunenviertel. Built in 1907, the eight interlinked *Höfe* reopened in 1996 with a congenial mix of cafes, galleries, boutiques and entertainment venues. The main entrance on Rosenthaler Strasse leads to **Court I**, prettily festooned with art nouveau tiles, while Court VII segues to the romantic **Rosenhöfe** with a sunken rose garden and tendril-like balustrades. (☑030-2809 8010; www.hackesche-hoefe. com; enter from Rosenthaler Strasse 40/41 or Sophienstrasse 6; admission free; ☑M1, ⑤Hackescher Markt, ⑪Weinmeisterstrasse)

Hamburger Bahnhof – Museum für Gegenwart
MUSEUM

2 Map p76, A3

Berlin's contemporary art showcase opened in 1996 in an old railway station, whose loft and grandeur are a great backdrop for this Aladdin's cave of paintings, installations, sculptures and video art. Changing exhibits span the arc of post-1950 artistic movements – from conceptual art and pop art to minimal art and Fluxus – and include seminal works by such major players as Andy Warhol, Cy Twombly, Joseph Beuys and Robert Rauschenberg. (Contemporary Art Museum; ☑030-266 424 242; www.smb.museum; Invalidenstrasse 50-51; adult/concession €14/7; ☑10am-6pm Tue, Wed & Fri, 10am-8pm Thu, 11am-6pm Sat & Sun; ☑M5, M8, M10, ⑤Hauptbahnhof, ⑪Hauptbahnhof)

Sammlung Boros
GALLERY

3 Map p76, B5

This Nazi-era bunker shelters one of Berlin's finest private contemporary art collections. Advertising guru Christian Boros acquired the behemoth in 2003 and converted it into a shining beacon of art. Book online (weeks, if not months, ahead!) to join a guided tour (also in English) of works by such hotshots as Wolfgang Tillmans, Olafur Eliasson and Ai Weiwei, and to pick up fascinating nuggets about the building's past incarnations. (Boros Collection; ☑030-2759 4065; www.sammlung-boros.de; Reinhardtstrasse 20; adult/concession €12/6; ☑tours 3-6.30pm Thu, 10am-6.30pm Fri-Sun; ☑M1, ⑤Friedrichstrasse, ⑪Oranienburger Tor, Friedrichstrasse)

Museum für Naturkunde
MUSEUM

4 Map p76, A3

Fossils and minerals don't quicken your pulse? Well, how about Tristan, one of the best-preserved *Tyrannosaurus rex* skeletons in the world, or the 12m-high *Brachiosaurus branchai,* the world's largest mounted dino skeleton? These Jurassic superstars are joined by a dozen other buddies, some of which are brought to virtual flesh-and-bone life with the help

Court I, Hackesche Höfe

of clever 'Juraskopes'. Other crowd favourites in this excellent museum include Knut, the world's most famous dead polar bear, and an ultrarare archaeopteryx. (Museum of Natural History; ☎030-2093 8591; www.naturkundemuseum. berlin; Invalidenstrasse 43; adult/concession incl audioguide €8/5; ◷9.30am-6pm Tue-Fri, 10am-6pm Sat & Sun; ☒M5, M8, M10, 12, ⓊNaturkundemuseum)

Neue Synagoge   SYNAGOGUE

5 ◎ Map p76, D5

The gleaming gold dome of the Neue Synagoge is the most visible symbol of Berlin's revitalised Jewish community. The 1866 original was Germany's largest synagogue but its modern incarnation is not so much a house of worship (although prayer services do take place), as a museum and place of remembrance called **Centrum Judaicum**. The dome can be climbed from April to September (adult/concession €3/2.50). An audioguide costs €3. (☎030-8802 8300; www.centrumjudaicum.de; Oranienburger Strasse 28-30; adult/concession €5/4; ◷10am-6pm Mon-Fri, to 7pm Sun, closes 3pm Fri & 6pm Sun Oct-Mar; ☒M1, ⓊOranienburger Tor, ⓈOranienburger Strasse)

KW Institute for Contemporary Art   GALLERY

6 ◎ Map p76, D4

In an old margarine factory, nonprofit KW helped ensure the fate of the

Understand
Jewish Berlin

Over the last quarter century, Berlin has had the fastest-growing Jewish community in the world. It is diverse: most members are Russian Jewish immigrants but there are also Jews of German heritage, young Israelis wishing to escape their politically frustrating homeland and American expats lured by Berlin's low-cost living and limitless creativity. There are no official numbers, but estimates suggest that there are around 45,000 Jewish residents in Berlin today. Germany in general now has the third-largest Jewish population in Europe, after Britain and France.

Community Roots

Records show that Jews first settled in Berlin in 1295, but throughout the Middle Ages they had to contend with being blamed for any kind of societal or economic woe. When the plague struck (1348–49), rumours that Jews had poisoned the wells led to the first major pogrom. In 1510, 38 Jews were publicly tortured and burned for allegedly stealing the host from a church because a confession by the actual (Christian) perpetrator was deemed too straightforward to be true. Financial inter- ests, not humanitarian ones, motivated the Elector Friedrich Wilhelm to invite Jewish families expelled from Vienna to settle in Berlin in 1671. To his credit, he later extended the offer to Jews in general and also allowed them to practise their faith – which at the time was still considered a privilege throughout Europe.

The Last Century

By the late 19th century, many of Berlin's Jews, numbering about 5% of the city's population, had become thoroughly German in speech and identity. When a wave of Hasidic Jews escaping the pogroms of Eastern Europe arrived around the same time, they found their way to today's Scheunenviertel, which at that time was an immigrant slum with cheap housing. By 1933 Berlin's Jewish population had grown to around 160,000 and constituted one-third of all Jews living in Germany. The well-known horrors of the Nazi years sent most into exile and left 55,000 dead. Only about 1000 to 2000 Jews are believed to have survived the war years in Berlin, often with the help of their non-Jewish neighbours.

Scheunenviertel as Berlin's original post-Wall art district. It continues to stage groundbreaking exhibits reflecting the latest – and often radical – trends in contemporary art. Reduced admission (€4) Thursday after 6pm with free tour at 6pm. (☎030-243 4590; www.kw-berlin.de; Auguststrasse 69; adult/concession €6/4; ☺noon-7pm Wed-Mon, to 9pm Thu; 🚋M1, Ⓢ Oranienburger Strasse, Ⓤ Oranienburger Tor)

Eating

House of Small Wonder
INTERNATIONAL €

7 🍴 Map p76, C5

A wrought-iron staircase spirals up to this whimsical brunch and lunch cafe where plants are potted in birdcages and the ceiling is made of opaque glass panels. The menu features comfort food inspired by American, Japanese and European tastes and includes sandwiches (top choice: avocado and goat's cheese), home-baked goods and such eccentric mains as Okinawan Taco Rice. (☎030-2758 2877; www.houseofsmallwonder.de; Johannisstrasse 20; dishes €4-11; ☺9am-5pm; 📶; Ⓤ Oranienburger Tor, Ⓢ Oranienburger Strasse, Friedrichstrasse)

Hummus & Friends
ISRAELI €

8 🍴 Map p76, D5

'Make Hummus, Not Walls' is the motto at this vegan and kosher kitchen next to the Neue Synagoge (p79). The eponymous chickpea dip, whipped up with special beans from Galilee, is naturally the menu star. Also try the paper-wrapped oven-roasted cauliflower with creamy tahini. (☎030-5547 1454; www.hummus-and-friends.com; Oranienburger Strasse 27; mains €7.50-8.50; ☺9.30am-midnight; 🚋M1, Ⓢ Oranienburger Strasse)

Chèn Chè
VIETNAMESE €€

9 🍴 Map p76, F4

In this exotic Vietnamese tearoom you can settle down in the charming Zen garden or beneath the hexagonal chandelier made from the torn pages of a herbal medicine book. The compact menu features healthy and meticulously presented *pho* (soups), curries and noodle dishes served in traditional clay pots. Exquisite tea selection and small shop. (☎030-2888 4282; www.chenche-berlin.de; Rosenthaler Strasse 13; dishes €6.50-11; ☺noon-midnight; 🍴; 🚋M1, Ⓤ Rosenthaler Platz)

Muret La Barba
ITALIAN €€

10 🍴 Map p76, F4

This wine shop–bar–restaurant combo oozes the kind of rustic authenticity that instantly transports cognoscenti to Italy. The food is hearty, inventive and made with top ingredients imported from the motherland. All wine is available by the glass or by the bottle (corkage fee €10). (☎030-2809 7212; www.muretlabarba.de; Rosenthaler Strasse 61; mains €12.50-25; ☺10am-midnight Mon-Fri, noon-midnight Sat & Sun; 🚋M1, Ⓤ Rosenthaler Platz)

Schwarzwaldstuben

GERMAN €€

11 Map p76, D4

In the mood for a Hansel and Gretel moment? Then join the other 'lost kids' for satisfying slow food from the southwest German regions of Baden and Swabia. Tuck into gut-filling platters of *spaetzle* (mac 'n' cheese), *Maultaschen* (ravioli-like pasta), giant schnitzel or a daily special. Dine amid rustic and tongue-in-cheek forest decor or grab a table on the pavement. (☏030-2809 8084; www.schwarzwaldstuben-berlin.com; Tucholskystrasse 48; mains €7-16; ☉9am-midnight; ☒M1, Ⓢ Oranienburger Strasse)

Local Life
Haus Schwarzenberg

The last holdout in the heavily gentrified area around the Hackescher Markt, **Haus Schwarzenberg** (www. haus-schwarzenberg.org; Rosenthaler Strasse 39; admission free; ☉courtyard 24hr; ☒M1, Ⓢ Hackescher Markt) is an unpretentious space where art and creativity are allowed to flourish beyond the mainstream and commerce. Festooned with street art and bizarre metal sculptures, the courtyards lead to studios, offices, the 'Monsterkabinett 'amusement park', the edgy-arty Eschschloraque Rümschrümp bar, a tiny arthouse cinema and a trio of exhibits dealing with Jewish persecution during the Third Reich.

Katz Orange

INTERNATIONAL €€€

12 Map p76, D2

With its gourmet, organic farm-to-table menu, stylish country flair and top-notch cocktails, the 'Orange Cat' hits a gastro grand slam. It will have you purring for such perennial faves as Duroc pork that's been slow-roasted for 12 hours (nicknamed 'candy on bone'). The setting in a castle-like former brewery is stunning, especially in summer when the patio opens. (☏030-983 208 430; www.katzorange.com; Bergstrasse 22; mains €18-29; ☉6-11pm; ☒M8, Ⓤ Rosenthaler Platz)

Pauly Saal

GERMAN €€€

13 Map p76, D4

Since taking the helm at this Michelin-starred outpost, Arne Anker has given the cuisine a youthful and lighter edge while still following the seasonal-regional credo. Only multicourse menus are served, even at lunch. Nothing has changed about the stunning venue: the edgy-art-decorated gym of a former Jewish girls' school in a Bauhaus building. On balmy days, sit beneath the old schoolyard's leafy trees. (☏030-3300 6070; www.paulysaal.com; Augustrasse 11-13; 2-/3-/4-course lunches €36/46/56, 4-/7-course dinners €76/97; ☉noon-2pm & 6-9.30pm Tue-Sat, bar to 2.30am; ☒M1, Ⓢ Oranienburger Strasse, Ⓤ Oranienburger Tor)

Drinking

Clärchens Ballhaus   CLUB

14  Map p76, E4

Yesteryear is right now at this late, great 19th-century dance hall where groovers and grannies hoof it across the parquet without even a touch of irony. There are different sounds nightly – salsa to swing, tango to disco – and a live band on Saturday. Dancing kicks off from 9pm or 9.30pm. Easy door but often packed, so book a table. (📞030-282 9295; www.ballhaus. de; Auguststrasse 24; ⊘11am-late; 🚊M1, Ⓢ Oranienburger Strasse)

Buck and Breck   COCKTAIL BAR

15  Map p76, E2

Liquid maestro Gonçalo de Sousa Monteiro and his team treat grown-up patrons to libational flights of fancy in their clandestine cocktail salon with classic yet friendly flair. Historical concoctions are a strength, including the eponymous bubbly-based cocktail Buck and Breck, named for mid-19th-century US president James Buchanan and his VP John Breckinridge. (www. buckandbreck.com; Brunnenstrasse 177; ⊘7pm-late; 🚊M1, Ⓤ Rosenthaler Platz)

Pier   PUB

16  Map p76, B2

Subtitled 'Badeanzüge & Bier' (Swimsuits & Beer), this upscale craft-beer bar was inspired by an 1865 Coney Island beach club serving beer. The

Clärchens Ballhaus

Berlin incarnation supplies the thirsty with a deftly curated changing roster of about 15 handmade draught beers plus about 30 bottled varieties. (📞030-6026 0714; www.the-pier.de; Invalidenstrasse 30; ⊘7pm-1am; Ⓤ Naturkundemuseum)

Kaffee Burger   CLUB

17  Map p76, H3

Nothing to do with either coffee or meat patties, this sweaty cult club with lovingly faded Communist-era decor is a fun-for-all concert and party pen. The sound policy swings from indie and electro to klezmer punk without missing a beat. Also has readings and poetry slams. (www.kaffeeburger.de; Torstrasse 60; ⊘from 9pm Mon-Thu, from 10pm Fri-Sun; Ⓤ Rosa-Luxemburg-Platz)

Entertainment

Chamäleon Varieté
CABARET

18 ⭐ Map p76, F5

A marriage of art nouveau charms and high-tech theatre trappings, this intimate 1920s-style venue in an old ballroom hosts classy variety shows – comedy, juggling acts and singing – often in sassy, sexy and unconventional fashion. (☎030-400 0590; www.chamaeleonberlin.com; Rosenthaler Strasse 40/41; tickets €29-69; 🚋M1, Ⓢ Hackescher Markt)

Friedrichstadt-Palast Berlin
CABARET

19 ⭐ Map p76, C5

Europe's largest revue theatre is coming up to its centenary and is still famous for glitzy-glam Vegas-style variety shows with leggy showgirls, singing, elaborate costuming, a high-tech stage, mind-boggling special effects and abundant artistry. Productions are innovative, highly professional and don't require German-language skills. (☎030-2326 2326; www.palast.berlin; Friedrichstrasse 107; tickets €17-120; 🚋M1, Ⓤ Oranienburger Tor, Ⓢ Friedrichstrasse, Oranienburger Strasse)

Shopping

Bonbonmacherei
FOOD

20 🔒 Map p76, D4

The aroma of peppermint and liquorice wafts through this old-fashioned basement candy kitchen whose owners use antique equipment and time-tested recipes to churn out such souvenir-worthy treats as their signature leaf-shaped Berliner Maiblätter made with woodruff. (☎030-4405 5243; www.bonbonmacherei.de; Oranienburger Strasse 32, Heckmann Höfe; ⊙noon-7pm Wed-Sat Sep-Jun; 🚋M1, Ⓢ Oranienburger Strasse)

Kauf Dich Glücklich
FASHION & ACCESSORIES

21 🔒 Map p76, F4

What began as a waffle cafe and vintage shop has turned into a small emporium of indie concept boutiques with this branch being the flagship. It's a prettily arranged and eclectic mix of reasonably priced accessories, music and clothing for him and her from the own-brand KDG-collection and other hand-picked, mostly Scandinavian and Berlin, labels. (✆030-2887 8817; www.kaufdichgluecklich-shop.de; Rosenthaler Strasse 17; ⏰11am-8pm Mon-Sat; Ⓤ Weinmeisterstrasse, Rosenthaler Platz)

Ampelmann Berlin
GIFTS & SOUVENIRS

22 🔒 Map p76, F5

It took a vociferous grass-roots campaign to save the little Ampelmann, the endearing fellow on East German pedestrian traffic lights. Now the beloved cult figure and global brand graces an entire shop's worth of T-shirts, fridge magnets, pasta, onesies, umbrellas and other knick-knacks. Check the website for additional branches around town. (✆030-4472 6438; www.ampelmann.de; Rosenthaler Strasse 40/41, Hackesche Höfe, Court V.; ⏰9.30am-9pm Mon-Sat, 1-8pm Sun; 🚋M1, Ⓢ Hackescher Markt, Ⓤ Weinmeisterstrasse)

⊙ Local Life
Sunday Concerts

From roughly September to June, clued-in classical music fans gather on Sunday evenings amid the faded elegance of the early 20th-century **Spiegelsaal** (✆030-5268 0256; www.sonntagskonzerte.de; Auguststrasse 24; adult/concession €12/8; ⏰Sep-Jun; 🚋M1, Ⓢ Oranienburger Strasse, Ⓤ Oranienburger Tor) (Mirror Hall) for piano concerts, opera recitals, string quartets and other musical offerings. It's upstairs from Clärchens Ballhaus. It's possible to make reservations online, but there are no assigned seats

1. Absinth Depot Berlin
FOOD & DRINKS

23 🔒 Map p76, G5

Van Gogh, Toulouse-Lautrec and Oscar Wilde are among the fin-de-siècle artists who drew inspiration from the 'green fairy', as absinthe is also known. This quaint little shop has over 100 varieties of the potent stuff and an expert owner who'll happily help you pick out the perfect bottle for your own mind-altering rendezvous. (✆030-281 6789; www.erstes-absinthdepotberlin.de; Weinmeisterstrasse 4; ⏰2pm-midnight Mon-Fri, 1pm-midnight Sat; Ⓤ Weinmeisterstrasse)

Explore

Kurfürstendamm

The glittering heart of West Berlin during the Cold War, Kurfürstendamm is a big draw for shopaholics, an irresistible blend of haute couture, high-street chains and department stores. Also venture into its side streets to sample the area's bourgeois charms, reflected in its palatial townhouses, distinctive indie shops, neighbourhood-adored restaurants, snazzy bars and Old Berlin–style pubs.

CLAUDIO DIVIZIA/SHUTTERSTOCK ©

The Sights in a Day

☀ There will be a lot of walking today, so gather some strength with a bountiful breakfast at **Café-Restaurant Wintergarten im Literaturhaus** (p93), a darling neighbourhood cafe. Thus fortified, get the scoop on Berlin's tumultuous past at the **Story of Berlin** (p90), then launch an extended shopping spree down the boulevard, perhaps pausing to ponder the futility of war at the **Kaiser-Wilhelm-Gedächtniskirche** (p90). Check out the snazzy concept mall **Bikini Berlin** (p97), then swing down to the grand department store **KaDeWe** (p96) for a late lunch in the glorious food hall.

☼ Do a bit more shopping if you must, or make your way to the **Museum für Fotografie** (p91) to look at Helmut Newton's nudes and whatever else is on view. Now it's practically beer o'clock and the beer garden tables at **Schleusenkrug** (p94) are singing their siren song.

☾ A fine place for dinner is **Restaurant Faubourg** (p94) or, if you're in the mood for authentic Chinese, **Good Friends** (p93). Alternatively, catch a show and a bite in the stunning mirrored tent of **Bar Jeder Vernunft** (p96).

 Best of Berlin

Music & Performance
Staatsoper im Schiller Theater (p96)

Bar Jeder Vernunft (p96)

A-Trane (p96)

Shopping
Bikini Berlin (p97)

KaDeWe (p96)

Käthe Wohlfahrt (p97)

Eating
Good Friends (p93)

Museums
Museum für Fotografie (p91)

Getting There

🚌 **Bus** Zoologischer Garten is the western terminus for buses 100 and 200.

Ⓢ **S-Bahn** Zoologischer Garten is the most central station.

Ⓤ **U-Bahn** The U1 stations Uhlandstrasse, Kurfürstendamm and Wittenbergplatz put you right into shopping central.

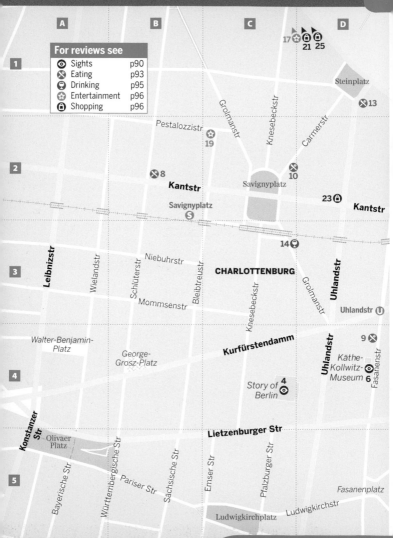

	A		B		C		D

For reviews see

◎	Sights	p90
⊗	Eating	p93
⊖	Drinking	p95
✪	Entertainment	p96
🔒	Shopping	p96

17 ✪ 21 🔒 25 🔒

Steinplatz

⊗ 13

Grolmanstr

Pestalozzistr
19 ✪

Knesebeckstr

Carmerstr

⊗ 8

Kantstr

10 ⊗

Savignyplatz

23 🔒

Kantstr

Savignyplatz
Ⓢ

14 ⊖

Leibnizstr

Wielandstr

Schlüterstr

Niebuhrstr

Bleibtreustr

CHARLOTTENBURG

Knesebeckstr

Grolmanstr

Uhlandstr

Uhlandstr Ⓤ

Mommsenstr

Kurfürstendamm

Uhlandstr

9 ⊗

Käthe-
Kollwitz-
Museum

Fasanenstr

6 ◎

Walter-Benjamin-
Platz

George-
Grosz-Platz

Story of
Berlin
4 ◎

Konstanzer Str

Olivaer
Platz

Lietzenburger Str

Bayerische Str

Württembergische Str

Pariser Str

Sachsische Str

Emser Str

Pfalzburger Str

Fasanenplatz

Ludwigkirchplatz

Ludwigkirchstr

E

Fasanenstr

Museum für
Fotografie

Hardenbergstr

Fasanenstr

C/O ◎3
Berlin

16 🚇

F

Jebensstr

5 ◎

🅁 Zoologischer
Garten

🅂

Zoologischer
Garten

🚇 Zoologischer
Garten

Budapester Str

🛑
11

G

Zoologischer
Garten

Hardenbergplatz

◎2
Berlin Zoo

Berlin Aquarium

22
🚇15

Breitscheidplatz

Kaiser-Wilhelm- ◎1
Gedächtniskirche

🛈

Berlin Tourist
Info -
Rankestrasse

Kurfürstendamm
🚇

🔒
24

🛑
12

Joachimstaler Str

Meinekestr

Rankeplatz

Rankestr

Eislebener Str

Lietzenburger Str

Schaperstr

⭐18

Los-
Angeles-
Platz

Marburger Str

Augsburger 🚇
Str

Nürnberger
Platz

Geisbergstr

H

N 0 ⬛ 200 m
0 0.1 miles

1

2

Olof-
Palme-Platz

◎7
Budapester
Str

Kurfürstenstr

Ansbacher Str

Europa-
Center

🛈 Berlin Tourist Info -
Europa-Center

Tauentzienstr

Nürnberger Str

An der Urania
Lietzenburger Str

Bamberger Str

Ansbacher Str

Fuggerstr

Welserstr

3

🔒
20

🚇 **4**
Wittenbergplatz

5

Sights

Kaiser-Wilhelm-
Gedächtniskirche   CHURCH

1 Map p88, G3

Allied bombing in 1943 left only the
husk of the west tower of this once
magnificent neo-Romanesque church
standing. Now an antiwar memorial,
it stands quiet and dignified amid the
roaring traffic. Historic photographs
displayed in the **Gedenkhalle** (Hall of
Remembrance), at the bottom of the
tower, help you visualise the former
grandeur of this 1895 church. The
adjacent octagonal hall of worship,
added in 1961, has glowing midnight-
blue glass walls and a giant 'floating'
Jesus. (Kaiser Wilhelm Memorial Church;
☑030-218 5023; www.gedaechtniskirche.
com; Breitscheidplatz; admission free;
☑church 9am-7pm, memorial hall 10am-6pm
Mon-Fri, 10am-5.30pm Sat, noon-5.30pm
Sun; ☐100, 200, ☑Zoologischer Garten,
Kurfürstendamm, ⓢZoologischer Garten)

Berlin Zoo   ZOO

2 Map p88, G2

Berlin's zoo holds a triple record as
Germany's oldest, most species-rich
and most popular animal park. It
was established in 1844 under King
Friedrich Wilhelm IV, who not only
donated the land but also pheasants
and other animals from the royal fam-
ily's private reserve on the Pfaueninsel. The menagerie includes 20,000
critters representing 1500 species,
including orangutans, koalas, rhinos,
giraffes and penguins. A popular
feature are the daily feeding sessions,
starting at 10.30am with the polar
bears. (☑030-254 010; www.zoo-berlin.de;
Hardenbergplatz 8; adult/child €14.50/7.50,
with aquarium €20/10; ☑9am-6.30pm Apr-
Sep, to 6pm Mar & Oct, to 4.30pm Nov-Feb;
☐100, 200, ⓢZoologischer Garten, ☑Zoolo-
gischer Garten, Kurfürstendamm)

C/O Berlin   GALLERY

3 Map p88, E2

The C/O Berlin is Berlin's most
respected private, nonprofit exhibition
centre for international photography.
Founded in 2000 it moved into its current digs in the historic Amerika Haus
near Zoo Station in 2014. Its roster
of highbrow exhibits has featured
many members of the shutterbug
elite, including Annie Leibovitz,
Stephen Shore, Nan Goldin and Anton
Corbijn. (☑030-284 441 662; www.co-
berlin.org; Amerika Haus, Hardenbergstrasse
22-24; adult/concession/under 18 €10/5/
free; ☑11am-8pm; ⓢZoologischer Garten,
☑Zoologischer Garten)

Story of Berlin   MUSEUM

4 Map p88, C4

This engaging museum breaks 800
years of Berlin history down into bite-
size chunks that are easy to swallow
but substantial enough to be satisfying. Each of the 23 rooms uses sound,
light, technology and original objects
to zero in on a specific theme or epoch
in the city's history, from its founding

OSCITY/SHUTTERSTOCK ©

Orangutan, Berlin Zoo

in 1237 to the fall of the Berlin Wall. The creepily fascinating climax is a tour (in English) of a still-functional atomic bunker beneath the building. (📞030-8872 0100; www.story-of-berlin.de; Kurfürstendamm 207-208, enter via Ku'damm Karree mall; adult/concession €12/9; ⏱10am-8pm, last admission 6pm; 🚌X9, X10, 109, 110, M19, M29, TXL, Ⓤ Uhlandstrasse)

Museum für Fotografie   MUSEUM

5 ◉ Map p88, F2

In a converted Prussian officers' casino, this museum showcases the artistic legacy of Helmut Newton (1920–2004), the Berlin-born *enfant terrible* of fashion and lifestyle photography, with the two lower floors

dedicated to his life and work. On the top floor, the gloriously restored barrel-vaulted **Kaisersaal** (Emperor's Hall) forms a grand backdrop for changing high-calibre photography exhibits drawn from the archive of the Kunstbibliothek (Art Library). (📞030-266 424 242; www.smb.museum/ mf; Jebensstrasse 2; adult/concession €10/5; ⏱10am-6pm Tue, Wed & Fri, 10am-8pm Thu, 11am-6pm Sat & Sun; Ⓢ Zoologischer Garten, Ⓤ Zoologischer Garten)

Käthe-Kollwitz-Museum   MUSEUM

6 ◉ Map p88, D4

This museum in a charming villa is devoted to German artist Käthe Kollwitz (1867–1945), whose social and

Understand
Berlin in the 'Golden' Twenties

The 1920s began as anything but golden, marked by a lost war, social and political instability, hyperinflation, hunger and disease. Many Berliners responded by behaving like there was no tomorrow and made their city as much a den of decadence as a cauldron of creativity. Cabaret, Dada and jazz flourished. Pleasure pits popped up everywhere, turning the city into a 'sextropolis' of Dionysian dimensions. Bursting with energy, it became a laboratory for anything new and modern, drawing giants of architecture (Hans Scharoun, Walter Gropius), fine arts (George Grosz, Max Beckmann) and literature (Bertolt Brecht, Christopher Isherwood).

Cafes & Cabaret

Cabarets provided a titillating fantasy of play and display where transvestites, singers, magicians, dancers and other entertainers made audiences forget the harsh realities. Kurfürstendamm evolved into a major nightlife hub with glamorous cinemas, theatres and restaurants. The Romanisches Café, on the site of today's Europa-Center, was practically the second living room for artists, actors, writers, photographers, film producers and other creative types, some famous, most not. German writer Erich Kästner even called it the 'waiting room of the talented'.

Celluloid History

The 1920s and early '30s were also a boom time for Berlin cinema, with Marlene Dietrich seducing the world and the mighty UFA studio producing virtually all of Germany's celluloid output. Fritz Lang, whose seminal works *Metropolis* (1926) and *M* (1931) brought him international fame, was among the dominant filmmakers.

The Crash

The fun came to an instant end when the US stock market crashed in 1929, plunging the world into economic depression. Within weeks, half a million Berliners were jobless, and riots and demonstrations again ruled the streets. The volatile, increasingly polarised political climate led to clashes between communists and the emerging NSDAP (Nazi Party), led by Adolf Hitler. Soon jackboots, Brownshirts, oppression and fear would dominate daily life in Germany.

political awareness lent a tortured power to her lithographs, graphics, woodcuts, sculptures and drawings. In the newly revamped four-floor exhibit, you first get to meet this extraordinary woman who lived in Berlin for 52 years, then study her artistic visions, including the powerful antihunger lithography *Brot!* (Bread!; 1924) and the woodcut series *Krieg* (War; 1922–23). (📞030-882 5210; www.kaethe-kollwitz.de; Fasanenstrasse 24; adult/concession/under 18 €6/3/free, audioguide €3; ⏰11am-6pm; Ⓤ Uhlandstrasse)

Berlin Aquarium AQUARIUM

8 Map p88, H2

Three floors of exotic fish, amphibians and reptiles await at this endearingly old-fashioned aquarium with its darkened halls and glowing tanks. Some of the specimens in the famous Crocodile Hall could be the stuff of nightmares, but dancing jellyfish, iridescent poison frogs and a real-life 'Nemo' bring smiles to young and old. (📞030-254 010; www.aquarium-berlin.de; Budapester Strasse 32; adult/child €14.50/7.50, incl zoo €20/10; ⏰9am-6pm; ♿; 🚌X9, Ⓢ Zoologischer Garten, Ⓤ Zoologischer Garten)

Eating

Good Friends CHINESE €€

8 Map p88, B2

Good Friends is widely considered Berlin's best Cantonese restaurant. The ducks dangling in the window are merely an overture to a menu long enough to confuse Confucius, including plenty of authentic homestyle dishes. If sea cucumber with fish belly proves too challenging, you can always fall back on sweet-and-sour pork or fried rice with shrimp. (📞030-313 2659; www.goodfriends-berlin.de; Kantstrasse 30; 2-course lunches €7, dinner mains €7-20; ⏰noon-1am; Ⓢ Savignyplatz)

Neni INTERNATIONAL €€

This bustling greenhouse-style dining hall at the 25hours Hotel Bikini Berlin – located on the same floor as Monkey Bar (see 15 Map p88, G2) – presents a spirited menu of meant-to-share dishes inspired by the cuisines of Morocco, Israel, Iran and Spain. Top billing goes to the homemade falafel, the Jerusalem platter, the Reuben sandwich and the chia lemon-curd crumble. The 10th-floor views of the zoo and the rooftops are a bonus. (📞030-120 221 200; www.neniberlin.de; Budapester Strasse 40; dishes €5-26; ⏰noon-11pm Mon-Fri, 12.30-11pm Sat & Sun; 🚌100, 200, Ⓢ Zoologischer Garten, Ⓤ Zoologischer Garten)

Café-Restaurant Wintergarten im Literaturhaus INTERNATIONAL €€

9 Map p88, D4

The hustle and bustle of Ku'damm is only a block away from this genteel art nouveau villa with attached literary salon and bookshop. Tuck into seasonal bistro cuisine amid elegant Old Berlin flair in the gracefully stucco-ornamented rooms or, if weather permits, in the idyllic garden. Breakfast is served until 2pm. (☎030-882 5414; www.literaturhaus-berlin. de/wintergarten-cafe-restaurant.html; Fasanenstrasse 23; mains €8-16; ⊙9am-midnight; 🖉; Ⓤ Uhlandstrasse)

Dicke Wirtin
GERMAN €€

10 🍴 Map p88, C2

Old Berlin charm oozes from every nook and cranny of this been-here-forever pub, which pours nine draught beers (including the superb Kloster Andechs) and nearly three dozen homemade schnapps varieties. Hearty local and German fare like smoked

KW/SHUTTERSTOCK ©

Bikini Berlin (p97)

veal dumplings, boiled eel, beef liver and pork roast keeps brains balanced. Bargain lunches, too. (☎030-312 4952; www.dicke-wirtin.de; Carmerstrasse 9; mains €6-16.50; ⊙11am-late; Ⓢ Savignyplatz)

Schleusenkrug
GERMAN €€

11 🍴 Map p88, F1

Sitting pretty on the edge of the Tiergarten, next to a canal lock, Schleusenkrug truly comes into its own during beer garden season. People from all walks of life hunker over big mugs and comfort food – from grilled sausages to *Flammkuche* (Alsatian pizza) and weekly specials. Breakfast is served until 2pm. (☎030-313 9909; www.schleusenkrug.de; Müller-Breslau-Strasse; mains €4-15; ⊙10am-midnight May-Sep, to 7pm Oct-Apr; Ⓢ Zoologischer Garten, Ⓤ Zoologischer Garten)

Restaurant Faubourg
FRENCH €€€

12 🍴 Map p88, E3

At this château-worthy French restaurant, head chef Felix Mielke applies punctilious artisanship to top-notch regional ingredients, creating intensely flavoured and beautifully plated dishes. For maximum palate exposure, put together a meal from the appetiser menu, although the mains – prepared either in classic or contemporary fashion – also command attention, as does the wine list. Gorgeous Bauhaus-inspired decor. (☎030-800 999 7700; www.sofitel-berlin-kurfurstendamm. com; Augsburger Strasse 41; mains €20-42; ⊙noon-11pm; Ⓤ Kurfürstendamm)

Restaurant am Steinplatz

GERMAN €€€

13 Map p88, D1

The 1920s gets a 21st-century make-over at this stylish outpost with an open kitchen where Marcus Zimmer feeds regional products into classic German and Berlin recipes. Even rustic beer-hall dishes such as *Eisbein* (boiled pork knuckle) are imaginatively reinterpreted and beautifully plated. A perennial favourite is the *Königsberger Klopse* (veal dumplings with capers, beetroot and mashed potatoes). (☑030-5544 447 053; www.hotelsteinplatz. com; Steinplatz 4; mains €18-38, 4-/5-course dinners €56/65; ☺noon-2.30pm & 6.30-10.30pm; ☂; ☒M45, ☒Ernst-Reuter-Platz, Zoologischer Garten, ⑤Zoologischer Garten)

Drinking

Diener Tattersall

PUB

14 Map p88, C3

In business for over a century, this Old Berlin haunt was taken over by German heavyweight champion Franz Diener in the 1950s and has since been one of West Berlin's preeminent artist pubs. From Billy Wilder to Harry Belafonte, they all came for beer and *Bulette* (meat patties), and left behind signed black-and-white photographs that grace Diener's walls to this day. (☑030-881 5329; www.diener-berlin.de; Grolmanstrasse 47; ☺6pm-2am; ⑤Savignyplatz)

Local Life

Little Asia

It's not quite Chinatown, but if you're in the mood for Asian food, head to Kantstrasse between Savignyplatz and Wilmersdorfer Strasse to find the city's densest concentration of authentic Chinese, Vietnamese and Thai restaurants, shops and soup kitchens. Many offer value-priced lunches.

Monkey Bar

BAR

15 Map p88, G2

On the 10th floor of the 25hours Hotel Bikini Berlin, this 'urban jungle' hot spot delivers fabulous views of the city and the Berlin Zoo. On balmy days, the sweeping terrace is a handy perch for sunset drinks selected from a menu that gives prominent nods to tiki concoctions (including the original Trader Vic's Mai Tai) and gin-based cocktail sorcery. (☑030-120 221 210; www.25hours-hotel.com; Budapester Strasse 40; ☺noon-1am Sun-Thu, to 2am Fri & Sat; ☂; ☒100, 200, ⑤Zoologischer Garten, ☒Zoologischer Garten)

Bar Zentral

COCKTAIL BAR

16 Map p88, E3

Even though palm trees decorate the walls, there's not a cocktail umbrella in sight at this elegant drinking den tucked into a brick-vaulted S-Bahn arch. Helmed by two Berlin bar gurus, it delivers the gamut of cocktail mainstays alongside adventurous

Top Tip

Bus Tour on the Cheap

It's a poorly kept secret that one of Berlin's best bargains is a self-guided city tour aboard bus 100 or 200, whose routes check off nearly every major sight in the city centre travelling between Zoo Station and Alexanderplatz for the price of a public transport ticket (tariff AB, €2.70). You can even get on and off within the two hours of its validity period as long as you continue in the same direction. If you plan to explore all day, a Tageskarte (day pass, €7) is your best bet.

new concoctions. (www.barzentral.de; Lotte-Lenya-Bogen 551; ⊙from 5pm; **S**Zoologischer Garten, **U**Zoologischer Garten, Kurfürstendamm)

Entertainment

Staatsoper im Schiller Theater

OPERA

17 ⭐ Map p88, C1

Point your highbrow compass towards the Daniel Barenboim–led Staatsoper, Berlin's top opera company. While its historic digs on Unter den Linden are getting a facelift, the high-calibre productions are staged at the Schiller Theater in Charlottenburg. All operas are sung in their original language. (☎030-2035 4455; www.staatsoper-berlin. de; Bismarckstrasse 110; tickets €18-230; **U**Ernst-Reuter-Platz)

Bar Jeder Vernunft

CABARET

18 ⭐ Map p88, E5

Life's still a cabaret at this intimate 1912 mirrored art nouveau tent, which puts on sophisticated song-and-dance shows, comedy and *chansons* nightly. Seating is in upholstered booths or at little cafe tables, both with waiter service. Many shows are suitable for patrons without German-language skills. (☎030-883 1582; www.bar-jeder-vernunft.de; Schaperstrasse 24; tickets €24.50; **U**Spichernstrasse)

A-Trane

JAZZ

19 ⭐ Map p88, C2

Herbie Hancock and Diana Krall have graced the stage of this intimate jazz club, but mostly it's emerging talent bringing their A-game to the A-Trane. Entry is free on Monday when local boy Andreas Schmidt and his band get everyone toe-tapping, and after midnight on Saturday for the late-night jam session. (☎030-313 2550; www.a-trane.de; Bleibtreustrasse 1; admission varies; ⊙8pm-1am Sun-Thu, to late Fri & Sat; **S**Savignyplatz)

Shopping

KaDeWe

DEPARTMENT STORE

20 Map p88, H4

Every day some 180,000 shoppers invade continental Europe's largest department store. Going strong since 1907, it boasts an assortment so vast that a pirate-style campaign is the best way to plunder its bounty. If pushed for time, at least hurry up to the legendary 6th-floor gourmet food hall. The name, by the way, stands for *Kaufhaus des Westens* (department store of the West). (☏030-212 10; www.kadewe.de; Tauentzienstrasse 21-24; ☺10am-8pm Mon-Thu, 10am-9pm Fri, 9.30am-8pm Sat; Ⓤ Wittenbergplatz)

Manufactum
HOMEWARES

21 🔒 Map p88, D1

Long before sustainable became a buzzword, this shop (the brainchild of a German Green Party member) stocked traditionally made quality products from around the world, many of which have stood the test of time. Cool finds include hand-forged iron pans by Turk, fountain pens by Pelikan and Japanese knives by Kenyo. (☏030-2403 3844; www.manufactum.de; Hardenbergstrasse 4-5; ☺10am-8pm Mon-Fri, to 6pm Sat; Ⓤ Ernst-Reuter-Platz)

Bikini Berlin
MALL

22 🔒 Map p88, G2

Germany's first concept mall opened in 2014 in a spectacularly rehabilitated 1950s architectural icon nicknamed 'Bikini' because of its design: 200m-long upper and lower sections separated by an open floor, now chastely covered by a glass facade. Inside are three floors of urban indie boutiques and short-lease pop-up 'boxes' that offer a platform for up-and-coming designers. (www.bikiniberlin.de; Budapester Strasse 38-50; ☺shops 10am-8pm Mon-Sat, building 9am-9pm Mon-Sat, 1-6pm Sun; 🚌; 🚌100, 200, Ⓤ Zoologischer Garten, Ⓢ Zoologischer Garten)

Stilwerk
HOMEWARES

23 🔒 Map p88, D2

This four-storey temple of good taste will have devotees of the finer things itching to redecorate. Everything you could possibly want for home and hearth is here – from key rings to grand pianos and vintage lamps – representing over 500 brands in 52 stores. (☏030-315 150; www.stilwerk.de/berlin; Kantstrasse 17; ☺10am-7pm Mon-Sat; Ⓢ Savignyplatz)

Käthe Wohlfahrt
ARTS & CRAFTS

24 🔒 Map p88, E3

With its mind-boggling assortment of traditional German Yuletide decorations and ornaments, this shop lets you celebrate Christmas year-round. It's accessed via a ramp that spirals around an 8m-high Christmas tree. (☏09861-4090; www.wohlfahrt.com; Kurfürstendamm 225-226; ☺10am-7pm Mon-Sat, 1-6pm Sun; Ⓤ Kurfürstendamm)

Berliner Trödelmarkt
MARKET

25 🔒 Map p88, D1

Vendors vie for your euros with yesteryear's fur coats, silverware, jewellery, lamps, dolls, hats and plenty of other stuff one might find in granny's attic. West of Tiergarten S-Bahn station, this is Berlin's oldest flea market (since 1973). The adjacent arts and crafts market sells mostly new stuff. (☏030-2655 0096; www.berliner-troedelmarkt.de; Strasse des 17 Juni; ☺10am-5pm Sat & Sun; Ⓢ Tiergarten)

Top Sights
Schloss Charlottenburg

Getting There

Schloss Charlotten-
burg is 3km northwest
of Zoologischer
Garten.

From Sophie-Charlotte-
Platz (U2) station it's
a scenic 1km walk via
Schlossstrasse or a ride
on bus 309.

Schloss Charlottenburg is an exquisite baroque palace and one of the few sites in Berlin that still reflects the one-time grandeur of the royal Hohenzollern clan, who ruled from 1415 until 1918. A visit is especially rewarding in summer when you can fold a stroll, sunbathing session or picnic by the carp pond into a day of peeking at royal treasures, including lavishly furnished period rooms and the largest collection of 18th-century French painting outside of France.

Neuer Flügel (New Wing), Schloss Charlottenburg

Don't Miss

Altes Schloss

The original royal living quarters in the baroque **Old Palace** are an extravaganza in stucco, brocade and overall opulence. Highlights include the Oak Gallery; the charming Oval Hall overlooking the park; Friedrich I's bedchamber, with the first-ever bathroom in a baroque palace; and the Eosander Chapel, with its *trompe l'œil* arches. Note that the Altes Schloss will be closed for renovation until at least 2017.

Neuer Flügel

Added under Frederick the Great, the **New Wing** (adult/concession incl tour or audioguide €10/7; ⏱10am-6pm Tue-Sun Apr-Oct, to 5pm Nov-Mar) contains the palace's most beautiful rooms, including the confection-like White Hall banquet room and the Golden Gallery, a rococo fantasy of mirrors and gilding. Other rooms show off paintings by such 18th-century French masters as Watteau and Pesne.

Schlossgarten

The expansive baroque gardens (admission free) linking the palace and the Spree River are part formal French, part unruly English and all idyllic playground. Wandering around the shady paths, lawns and carp pond, you'll eventually stumble upon the sombre Mausoleum and the charming Belvedere mini-palace.

Belvedere

This pint-size late-rococo **palace** (adult/concession €4/3; ⏱10am-6pm Tue-Sun Apr-Oct), built in 1788 as a teahouse for King Friedrich Wilhelm II, today makes an elegant setting for porcelain masterpieces by the royal manufacturer KPM, including lavish dinnerware services.

☎030-320 910

www.spsg.de

Spandauer Damm 10-22

day passes to all 4 buildings adult/concession €12/9

⏱hours vary by building

🚌M45, 109, 309, Ⓤ Richard-Wagner-Platz, Sophie-Charlotte-Platz

☑ Top Tips

▶ The Ticket charlottenburg+ (adult/concession €12/9) is a day pass valid for one-day admission to every open building.

▶ Arrive early, especially on weekends and in summer when queues can be long.

▶ A palace visit is easily combined with a spin around the trio of adjacent art museums.

✕ Take a Break

For a hearty meal and a cold beer, report to **Brauhaus Lemke** (☎030-3087 8979; Luisenplatz 1; mains €7-18; ⏱noon-midnight), a short walk from the palace.

Schloss Charlottenburg started out rather modestly as a petite summer retreat built for Sophie-Charlotte, wife of Elector Friedrich III. It was expanded in the mode of Versailles after the elector's self-promotion to king in 1701. Subsequent royals dabbled with the compound, most notably Frederick the Great who added the spectacular Neuer Flügel. The Neuer Pavillon, the Mausoleum and the Belvedere in the palace gardens date from the 19th century.

Neuer Pavillon

This Karl Friedrich Schinkel–designed **palace** (adult/concession incl audioguide €4/3; ☉10am-6pm Tue-Sun Apr-Oct, to 5pm Nov-Mar) was originally a royal summer retreat modelled on neoclassical Italian villas. Today, it shows off paintings and sculpture from the Romantic and Biedermeier periods.

Mausoleum

The temple-shaped 1810 **Mausoleum** (adult/concession €2/1; ☉10am-6pm Tue-Sun Apr-Oct) was conceived as the resting place of Queen Luise but was twice expanded to make room for other royals. Their marble sarcophagi are exquisitely sculpted works of art.

Nearby: Museum Berggruen

Picasso is especially well represented, with paintings, drawings and sculptures from all his major creative phases, at this delightful **museum** (☎030-266 424 242; www.smb.museum/mb; Schlossstrasse 1; adult/concession incl Sammlung Scharf-Gerstenberg €10/5; ☉10am-6pm Tue-Fri, 11am-6pm Sat & Sun). Elsewhere it's off to Paul Klee's emotional world, Henri Matisse's paper cut-outs, Alberto Giacometti's skinny sculptures and a sprinkling of African art that inspired them all.

Nearby: Sammlung Scharf-Gerstenberg

Surrealist art, including large bodies of work by René Magritte and Max Ernst alongside dreamscapes by Salvador Dalí and Jean Dubuffet, is the ammo of this **museum** (☎030-266 424 242; www.smb.museum/ssg; Schlossstrasse 70; adult/concession incl Museum Berggruen €10/5; ☉10am-6pm Tue-Fri, 11am-6pm Sat & Sun). Standouts among their 18th-century forerunners include Francisco Goya's spooky etchings and the creepy dungeon scenes by Italian engraver Giovanni Battista Piranesi.

Nearby: Bröhan Museum

This fine **museum** (☎030-3269 0600; www.broehan-museum.de; Schlossstrasse 1a; adult/concession/under 18 €8/5/free; ☉10am-6pm Tue-Sun) trains the spotlight on applied arts from the late 19th century until the outbreak of WWII. Pride of place goes to the art nouveau collection, with period rooms, furniture, porcelain and glass art from England, France, Germany, Scandinavia and Austria. A picture gallery with works by Berlin Secession artists complements the exhibits.

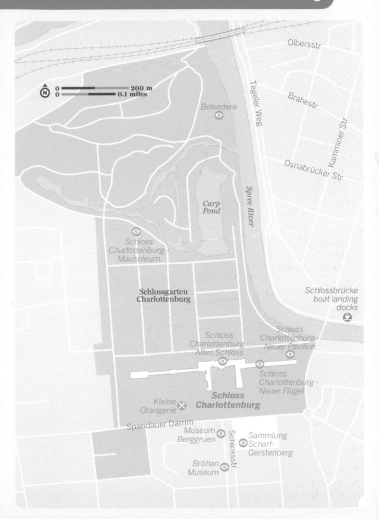

Olbersstr

Brahestr

Tegeler Weg

Kamminer Str

Osnabrücker Str

Belvedere

Spree River

Carp Pond

Schloss Charlottenburg - Mausoleum

Schlossgarten Charlottenburg

Schlossbrücke boat landing docks

Schloss Charlottenburg - Altes Schloss

Schloss Charlottenburg - Neuer Pavillon

Schloss Charlottenburg

Schloss Charlottenburg - Neuer Flügel

Kleine Orangerie

Spandauer Damm

Museum Berggruen

Schlossstr

Sammlung Scharf-Gerstenberg

Bröhan Museum

0   200 m
0   0.1 miles

Local Life
A Leisurely Saunter Through Schöneberg

Getting There

Schöneberg is wedged between Kurfürsten-damm and Kreuzberg.

U **U-Bahn** This itinerary is bookended by two stations: Viktoria-Luise-Platz (U4) and Kleistpark (U7).

Schöneberg flaunts a mellow middle-class identity but has a radical pedigree rooted in the squatter days of the '80s. Its multifaceted character nicely unfolds as you stroll from bourgeois Viktoria-Luise-Platz through Berlin's original gay quarter and along streets packed tight with boho cafes and smartly curated indie boutiques, to wind up at ethnically flavoured Hauptstrasse where David Bowie bunked back in the 1970s. A flurry of neighbourhood restaurants makes the area worth coming back to at night.

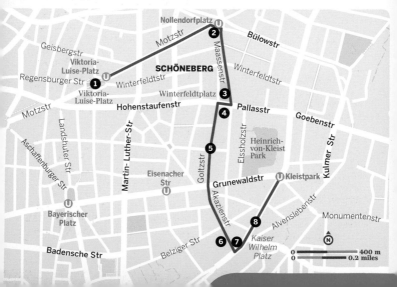

❶ Viktoria-Luise-Platz

Schöneberg's prettiest **square** is a symphony of flower beds, big old trees, a lusty fountain and benches where locals swap gossip or watch kids at play. It's framed by inviting cafes and 19th-century townhouses; note the ornate facades at Nos 7, 12 and 12a.

❷ Nollendorfplatz & the 'Gay Village'

Nollendorfplatz has been the gateway to Berlin's historic **gay quarter** since the 1920s, when Christopher Isherwood penned *Berlin Stories* (which inspired *Cabaret*) while living at Nollendorfstrasse 17. Rainbow flags still fly proudly above bars and businesses, especially along Motzstrasse and Fuggerstrasse. A memorial plaque at the U-Bahn station commemorates Nazi-era LGBT victims.

❸ Farmers Market

If it's Wednesday or Saturday morning, you're in luck because ho-hum **Winterfeldtplatz** erupts with farm-fresh fare. Along with seasonal produce you'll find handmade cheeses, cured meats, olives, local honey and plenty more staples and surprises. Saturday also has artsy-craftsy stalls.

❹ Chocophile Alert

Winterfeldt Schokoladen (☏030-2362 3256; www.winterfeldt-schokoladen.de; Goltzstrasse 23; ☺9am-8pm Mon-Fri, 9am-6pm Sat, noon-7pm Sun; Ⓤ Nollendorfplatz) stocks a vast range of international handmade gourmet chocolates, all displayed gallery-style in the original oak fixtures of a 19th-century pharmacy that doubles as a cafe.

❺ Boutique-Hopping

Goltzstrasse and its extension **Akazienstrasse** teem with indie boutiques selling vintage threads, slinky underwear and handmade jewellery, exotic teas and cooking supplies. No high-street chain in sight! Casual eateries and cafes abound.

❻ Double Eye

Javaholics cherish the award-winning espresso of **Double Eye** (Akazienstrasse 22; ☺8.30am-6.30pm Mon-Fri, 9am-6pm Sat; Ⓤ Eisenacher Strasse), which is why no one minds the inevitable queue.

❼ Möve im Felsenkeller

An artist hang-out since the 1920s, this cosy **pub** (☏030-781 3447; Akazienstrasse 2; ☺4pm-1am Mon-Fri, noon-2am Sat; Ⓤ Eisenacher Strasse) was where Jeffrey Eugenides penned his 2002 Pulitzer Prize–winning novel, *Middlesex*. A stuffed seagull dangling from the ceiling keeps an eye on patrons seeking inspiration from eight beers on tap.

❽ Hauptstrasse

The Turkish supermarket **Öz-Gida** (☏030-7871 5291; www.ozgida.de; Hauptstrasse 16; ☺8am-8pm Mon-Sat; Ⓤ Kleistpark) is known citywide for its olive selection, cheese spreads and quality meats. David Bowie and Iggy Pop shared a pad at Hauptstrasse 155. Look for the commemorative plaque.

Explore

Kreuzberg

Kreuzberg is the epicentre of free-wheeling, multicultural and alternative Berlin, especially in its eastern reaches between Moritzplatz and the Spree River. Come here to track down fabulous street art, scarf a doner kebab, browse vintage stores and hang by the canal, then find out why Kreuzberg is also known as a night-crawler's paradise. All that hipness has also spilled to the northern part of Neukölln.

The Sights in a Day

☀ If it's a warm and sunny summer day, a classic way to kick off a Kreuzberg sojourn is at the **Badeschiff** (p110). Put in a few hours of tanning, swimming and chilling at this riverside beach and swimming pool. Once you've had your relaxation fill, walk north on Schlesische Strasse, taking in the large-scale street art of Blu before joining the queue at **Burgermeister** (p110) for fist-sized burgers and homemade dips.

☀ After your refuelling stop, check out more **street art** (p113) along Skalitzer Strasse, then follow Oranienstrasse north, browsing shops like **VooStore** (p115) for streetwear, knick-knacks and vintage fashions. Study the local boho crowd over coffee (or the first beer of the day) at **Luzia** (p107).

🌙 After dark is when Kreuzberg truly comes alive. There's no shortage of doner kebab joints but if you prefer a sit-down dinner, good choices range from haute cuisine at **Restaurant Richard** (p111) to rib-sticking German classics at **Max und Moritz** (p110) and Turkish fare at **Defne** (p110). Thus fortified, you'll be ready to launch your dedicated study of Kreuzberg's bar scene.

For a local's day in Kreuzberg, see p106.

🔍 Local Life
Kotti Bar-Hop (p106)

❤ Best of Berlin
Eating
Max und Moritz (p110)
Burgermeister (p110)
Restaurant Richard (p111)

Bars
Hopfenreich (p113)
Schwarze Traube (p112)
Würgeengel (p107)
Club der Visionäre (p112)
Otto Rink (p107)

Gay & Lesbian
Roses (p107)
Möbel Olfe (p106)

Getting There

🚌 **Bus** M29 links Potsdamer Platz with Oranienstrasse via Checkpoint Charlie; the M41 (also coming from Potsdamer Platz) hits the Bergmannkiez before trudging down to Neukölln via Hermannplatz.

Ⓤ **U-Bahn** Getting off at Kottbusser Tor (U8) puts you in the thick of eastern Kreuzberg, although Görlitzer Bahnhof and Schlesisches Tor (U1) are also handy. For the Bergmannkiez area, head to Mehringdamm (U6) or Gneisenaustrasse (U7).

Local Life
Kotti Bar-Hop

Noisy, chaotic and sleepless, the area around Kottbusser Tor U-Bahn station (Kotti, for short) defiantly retains the punky-funky alt feel that's defined it since the 1970s. More gritty than pretty, this beehive of snack shops, cafes, pubs and bars is a launch step into some of the city's most hot-stepping nighttime action and is tailor-made for dedicated bar-hopping.

❶ Funky Salon

Tucked behind a pile of Turkish kebab shops, grocers and shisha bars, **Möbel Olfe** (📞030-2327 4690; www.moebel-olfe. de; Reichenberger Strasse 177; ⊙6pm-3am or later Tue-Sun) is a queer-leaning drinking saloon that channels the area's alternative vibe with boho decor, strong Polish beers and a chatty vibe.

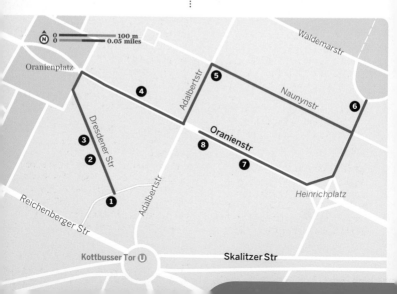

2 Grape Delights

Great for earlier in the evening, **Otto Rink** (www.ottorink.de; Dresdener Strasse 124; ⊘6pm-2am or later Mon-Sat) is an easy-going place to discover just how wonderful German wines can be. There's an emphasis on white varietals from the Moselle region, but wines from other German areas also feature on the menu.

3 1950s Cocktail Cave

If it's transcendent cocktails you're lusting after, point the compass to **Würgeengel** (☎030-615 5560; www. wuergeengel.de; Dresdener Strasse 122; ⊘7pm-2am or later), a stylish art-deco-style bar with chandeliers and shiny black surfaces. The name pays homage to the surreal 1962 Buñuel movie *Exterminating Angel*.

4 Luscious Lair

A fixture on Kreuzberg's hipster circuit, the vintage decor at **Luzia** (☎030-8179 9958; www.facebook.com/ luziabar; Oranienstrasse 34; ⊘noon-5am) gets updated with a mural by street artist Chin Chin. It's a comfy spot with lighting that gives even pasty-faced hipsters a glow. There's a smokers' lounge.

5 Gateway to Hell

Popular with punks and alternative types, the **Trinkteufel** (Drink Devil; ☎030-614 7128; www.trinkteufel.de; Naunynstrasse 60; ⊘1pm-4am Mon-Thu, 24hr Fri-Sun) is the dive bar where Pete Doherty downed a few before getting briefly arrested in 2009 after smashing a car window. Ponder this as you hang out by the bar and check out the trippy decor while swilling a cold brew.

6 Easy Medicine

Whatever ails you may well be fixed after dropping by the **Apotheken Bar** (☎030-6951 8108; www.apothekenbar.de; Mariannenplatz 6; ⊘7pm-2am Mon, 6pm-2am Tue-Thu, 6pm-4am Fri & Sat), a vintage-styled outpost in a 19th-century pharmacy. The original fixtures and old objects like a scale, bottles and signs form the atmospheric setting for expert cocktails, some featuring home-made tonic water and other potions.

7 Camp of Glam

A mashup of trash, camp and fun, **Roses** (☎030-615 6570; Oranienstrasse 187; ⊘9pm-6am or later) is a beloved pit stop for queers and their friends. Don't let the furry walls and a predominance of the colour pink distract you from the fact that this place takes drinking seriously until the early morning hours.

8 Burlesque Boite

A jewel-box-sized burlesque bar, **Prinzipal** (☎030-6162 7326; www. prinzipal-kreuzberg.com; Oranienstrasse 178; ⊘8pm-3am or later Mon-Sat) celebrates the glamour of the Golden Twenties with plenty of eye-candy detail, an apothecary-style bar and servers in custom-designed corsets.

A B C D

1

Heinrich-
Heine-
Platz

Leuschnerdamm

Engeldamm

Bethaniendamm

Waldemarstr

Mariannenplatz

Dresener Str

Muskauer Str

Manteuffelstr

Oranienstr
3

Oranienplatz

Dresener Str

Adalbertstr

2
10

Reichenberger Str

17
Oranienstr

Naunynstr

Heinrichplatz

Wassertorplatz

Kottbusser
Tor

Skalitzer Str

Görlitzer
Bahnhof

Spreewaldplatz

3
16

KREUZBERG

15

Admiralstr

Mariannenstr

18

Manteuffelstr

Lausitzer Str

Reichenberger Str

Ohlauer Str

Fraenkelufer

11

Paul-Lincke-Ufer

Urbanhafen

Planufer 4

Kottbusser Damm

Maybachufer

Landwehrkanal

4

Grimmstr

Böckhstr

Bürknerstr

Dieffenbachstr

Schönleinstr

Sanderstr

Hobrechtstr

Friedelstr

KREUZKÖLLN

5

Fichtestr

Hohenstaufenplatz

Pflügerstr

Friedelstr

Nansenstr

Urbanstr

Reuterplatz

For reviews see

⊙ Sights	p110
⊗ Eating	p110
⊜ Drinking	p112
★ Entertainment	p115
⌂ Shopping	p115

Sights

Badeschiff
SWIMMING

 1 Map p108, H4

Take an old river barge, fill it with water, moor it in the Spree and – voila! – an artist-designed urban lifestyle pool that is a popular swim-and-chill spot. With music blaring, a sandy beach, wooden decks, lots of hot bods and a bar to fuel the fun, the vibe is distinctly 'Ibiza on the Spree'. Come early on scorching days as it's often filled to capacity (1500 people max) by noon. Or show up for sunset and night-time parties or concerts. (☑030-533 2030; www.arena-berlin.de; Eichenstrasse 4; adult/concession €5/3; ☺8am-midnight May-Sep; ☒265, ☒Treptower Park, ☒Schlesische Strasse)

Eating

Burgermeister
BURGERS €

2 Map p108, F2

It's green, ornate, a century old and... it used to be a toilet. Now it's a burger joint beneath the elevated U-Bahn tracks. Get in line for the plump all-beef patties (try the Meisterburger with fried onions, bacon and barbecue sauce) paired with cheese fries and such homemade dips as peanut or mango curry. (☑030-2388 3840; www.burger-meister.de; Oberbaumstrasse 8; burgers €3.50-4.80; ☺11am-3am Sun-Thu, to 4am Fri & Sat; ☒Schlesisches Tor)

Max und Moritz
GERMAN €€

3 Map p108, A2

The patina of yesteryear hangs over this ode to old-school brewpub named for the cheeky Wilhelm Busch cartoon characters. Since 1902 it has packed hungry diners and drinkers into its rustic tile-and-stucco ornamented rooms for sudsy home brews and granny-style Berlin fare. A menu favourite is the *Königsberger Klopse* (veal meatballs in caper sauce). (☑030-6951 5911; www.maxundmoritzberlin. de; Oranienstrasse 162; mains €9.50-17; ☺5pm-midnight; ☎; ☒Moritzplatz)

Defne
TURKISH €€

4 Map p108, B4

If you thought Turkish cuisine stopped at the doner kebab, canal-side Defne will teach you otherwise. The appetiser platter alone elicits intense cravings (fabulous walnut-chilli paste!), but inventive mains such as *ali nacik* (sliced lamb with puréed eggplant and yoghurt) also warrant repeat visits. Good vegetarian choices too. Lovely summer terrace. (☑030-8179 7111; www.defne-restaurant.de; Planufer 92c; mains €8.50-20; ☺4pm-1am Apr-Sep, 5pm-1am Oct-Mar; ☒; ☒Kottbusser Tor, Schönleinstrasse)

Freischwimmer
INTERNATIONAL €€

5 Map p108, H3

In fine weather, few places are more idyllic than this rustic 1930s boathouse turned canal-side chill zone. The menu

Badeschiff

runs from meat and fish cooked on a lava rock grill to crisp salads, *Flamme-kuche* (French pizza) and seasonal specials. It's also a popular Sunday brunch spot (€12.90). Kayak and pedal boat rentals available. (☏030-6107 4309; www.freischwimmer-berlin.com; Vor dem Schlesischen Tor 2a; mains €10-16; ⊗noon-late Mon-Fri, 10am-late Sat & Sun; ☏; ⑤Treptower Park, ⑪Schlesisches Tor)

Restaurant Richard FRENCH €€€

6 🍴 Map p108, E1

A venue where Nazis partied in the 1930s and leftists debated in the '70s has been reborn as a fine-dining shrine solidly rooted in the French tradition and, since 2015, endowed

with a Michelin star. With its coffered ceiling, bubble chandeliers and risqué canvases, the decor is as luscious as the fancy food while the vibe remains charmingly relaxed. (☏030-4920 7242; www.restaurant-richard.de; Köpenicker Strasse 171; 4-course dinner €58, additional courses €10; ⊗7pm-midnight Tue-Sat; ⑪Schlesisches Tor)

eins44 FRENCH, GERMAN €€€

7 🍴 Map p108, E5

This outpost in a late 19th-century distillery serves 'elevated Franco-German bistro fare' that ticks all the boxes from old-fashioned to post-modern. Metal lamps, tiles and heavy wooden tables create industrial charm enhanced by large black-and-white photos. Lunches feature just a few classic dishes, while dinners are more elaborate. (☏030-6298 1212; www.eins44. com; Elbestrasse 28/29, 2nd courtyard; mains lunch €8-10, dinner €26, 3-/4-/5-course dinner €43/53/63; ⏱12.30-2.30pm Tue-Fri, 7pm-midnight Tue-Sat; 🛜; 🚌M41, 104, 167, Ⓤ Rathaus Neukölln)

Drinking

Schwarze Traube   COCKTAIL BAR

8 Map p108, E2

Mixologist Atalay Aktas was Germany's Best Bartender of 2013 and this pint-sized drinking parlour is where he and his staff create their magic potions. Since there's no menu, each drink is calibrated to the taste and mood of each patron using

premium spirits, expertise and a dash of psychology. (☏030-2313 5569; www.schwarzetraube.de; Wrangelstrasse 24; ⏱7pm-2am Sun-Thu, to 5am Fri & Sat; Ⓤ Görlitzer Bahnhof)

Club der Visionäre   CLUB

9 Map p108, H4

It's cold beer, crispy pizza and fine electro at this summertime day-to-night-and-back-to-day chill and party playground in an old canal-side boatshed. Park yourself beneath the weeping willows, stake out some turf on the upstairs deck or hit the tiny dance floor. To keep the party going year-round, CDV has expanded to the Hoppetosse boat moored nearby in the Spree. (☏030-6951 8942; www. clubdervisionaere.com; Am Flutgraben 1; ⏱3pm-late Mon-Fri, noon-late Sat & Sun; Ⓢ Treptower Park, Ⓤ Schlesisches Tor)

Ritter Butzke   CLUB

10 Map p108, A2

Ritter Butzke is a former bathroom fittings factory turned Kreuzberg party circuit fixture. Wrinkle-free hipsters hit the four floors for high-quality electronic music spun by both DJ legends and the latest sound spinners of the deep house and techno scenes. Thanks to the DonnersDuck party session, the Butzke weekend starts on Thursday. (www.ritterbutzke. de; Ritterstrasse 24; ⏱midnight-late Thu-Sat; Ⓤ Moritzplatz)

Ankerklause
PUB

11 Map p108, B4

Ahoy there! Drop anchor at this nautical kitsch tavern in an old harbour master's shack and enjoy the arse-kicking jukebox, cold beers and surprisingly good German pub fare. The best seats are on the geranium-festooned terrace where you can wave to the boats puttering along the canal. A cult pit stop until the wee hours. (030-693 5649; www.ankerklause.de; Kottbusser Damm 104; from 4pm Mon, from 10am Tue-Sun; Schönleinstrasse)

Hopfenreich
PUB

12 Map p108, F3

Berlin's first dedicated craft-beer bar has a changing roster of 22 global ales, IPAs and other brews on tap, including local heroes Heidenpeters and Hops & Barley, plus dozens of bottled varieties, both known and obscure. It's all served with hipster flourish in a corner pub near the Schlesische Strasse party mile. Tastings, tap takeovers and guest brewers keep things in flux. (030-8806 1080; www.hopfenreich.de; Sorauer Strasse 31; 4pm-2am Mon-Thu, to 3am Fri-Sun; Schlesisches Tor)

Watergate
CLUB

13 Map p108, G2

For a short night's journey into day, check into this high-octane riverside club with two floors, panoramic windows and a floating terrace overlooking the Oberbaumbrücke and Universal Music. Top DJs keep electro-hungry hipsters hot and sweaty till way past sunrise. Long queues, tight door. (030-6128 0394; www.water-gate.de; Falckensteinstrasse 49a; midnight-5am or later Wed, Fri & Sat; Schlesisches Tor)

Understand
Street Art

Berlin has emerged as European street-art capital where some major international artists including Blu, JR and Os Gemeos have left their mark on the city alongside local top talents such as Alias, El Bocho and XOOOOX. The area around U-Bahn station Schlesisches Tor has some house-wall-size classics, including *Pink Man* by Blu (next to Watergate) and *Yellow Man* by the Brazilian twins Os Gemeos on Oppelner Strasse. Skalitzer Strasse is also a fertile hunting ground, with Victor Ash's *Astronaut* and ROA's *Nature Morte* being highlights. Across the Spree River, the RAW Gelände (p126) party hub is an ever-changing canvas as is the courtyard of Haus Schwarzenberg (p82) in the Scheunenviertel. Alternative Berlin Tours (p158) runs an excellent street art tour with hands-on workshop.

Understand

Sounds of Berlin

Since the end of WWII, Berlin has spearheaded many of Germany's popular-music innovations. In West Berlin, Tangerine Dream helped to propagate the psychedelic sound of the late 1960s, while Ton Steine Scherben, led by Rio Reiser, became a seminal German-language rock band in the '70s and early '80s. Around the same time, Kreuzberg's sub-culture launched the punk movement at SO36 and other famous clubs. Regular visitors included the late David Bowie, who lived in Schöneberg in the 1970s and recorded his Berlin Trilogy *(Low, Heroes, Lodger)* at the famous Hansa Studios.

In the '80s, punk diva Nina Hagen helped chart the course for Neue Deutsche Welle (German New Wave) with such protagonists as DAF, Trio, Neonbabies, Ideal and UKW, as well as Rockhaus in East Berlin. Other seminal bands founded in the '80s are Die Ärzte and Einstürzende Neubauten who pioneered a proto-industrial sound that transformed oil drums, electric drills and chainsaws into musical instruments. Its founder Blixa Bargeld joined the Bad Seeds, helmed by Nick Cave who spent some heroin-addled time in Berlin in the early 1980s.

In East Germany, access to Western rock and other popular music was restricted, and few Western stars were invited to perform live. The artistic freedom of East German talent was greatly compromised as all lyrics had to be approved and performances were routinely monitored. Some *Ostrock* (eastern rock) bands like the Puhdys, Karat, Silly and City still managed to build up huge followings on both sides of the Wall. The small but vital East Berlin punk scene produced Sandow and Feeling B, members of whom went on to form the industrial metal band Rammstein in 1994, still Germany's top musical export.

Since the 1990s, electronic beats have shaped the Berlin sound, spawned a near-mythical club culture and defined the capital's cool factor. What today is a huge industry germinated in a dark and dank cellar club called UFO back in 1988 where the scene's 'godfathers' – Dr Motte, Westbam and Kid Paul – played their first gigs. It was Motte who came up with the idea to take the party to the street with a truck, loud beats and a bunch of friends dancing behind it – thus, the Love Parade was born (it peaked in 1999 with dozens of trucks and 1.5 million ravers swarming Berlin's streets).

Entertainment

Lido
LIVE MUSIC

14 Map p108, G3

A 1950s cinema has been recycled into a rock-indie-electro-pop mecca with mosh-pit electricity and a crowd that cares more about the music than about looking good. Global DJs and talented upwardly mobile live noise-makers pull in the punters. Its monthly Balkanbeats party is legendary. (☏030-6956 6840; www.lido-berlin.de; Cuvrystrasse 7; ⓤSchlesisches Tor)

Wild at Heart
LIVE MUSIC

15 ⭐ Map p108, D3

Named after a David Lynch road movie, this kitsch-cool dive with blood-red walls, tiki gods and Elvis paraphernalia hammers home punk, ska, surf-rock and rockabilly. It's really, REALLY loud, so if your ears need a break, head to the tiki-themed restaurant-bar next door. Free concerts on Wednesday. (☏030-611 9231; www.wildatheartberlin.de; Wiener Strasse 20; ⓥfrom 8pm Thu-Sat; ⓤGörlitzer Bahnhof)

Shopping

Hallesches Haus
HOMEWARES

16 🔒 Map p108, A3

IKEA graduates with a mod penchant will go ga-ga at this pretty pad packed with stylish whimsies for the home.

Even day-to-day items get a zany twist in this airy space converted from an old post office. The in-store cafe serves locally roasted coffee, baked goods and light meals at lunchtime, much of it organic and local. (www.hallescheshaus.com; Tempelhofer Ufer 1; ⓥ9am-7pm Mon-Fri, 11am-4pm Sat; ⓤHallesches Tor)

VooStore
FASHION & ACCESSORIES

17 🔒 Map p108, B2

Kreuzberg's first concept store opened in an old backyard locksmith shop off gritty Oranienstrasse, stocking style-forward designer threads and accessories by such crave-worthy labels as Acne Studios, Soulland, Henrik Vibskov, Carven and dozens more, along with tightly curated books, gadgets, mags and spirits. The in-house cafe is a nice touch. (☏030-6957 972 710; www.vooberlin.com; Oranienstrasse 24; ⓥ10am-8pm Mon-Sat; ⓤKottbusser Tor)

Hard Wax
MUSIC

18 🔒 Map p108, B3

This well hidden outpost has been on the cutting edge of electronic music for about two decades and is a must-stop for fans of techno, house, minimal, dubstep and whatever permutation comes along next. (☏030-6113 0111; www.hardwax.com; Paul-Lincke-Ufer 44a, 3rd fl, door A, 2nd courtyard; ⓥnoon-8pm Mon-Sat; ⓤKottbusser Tor)

Local Life
Nosing Around Neukölln

Getting There

Neukölln is just south of Kreuzberg, separated from it by the Landwehrkanal.

U **U-Bahn** Start at Schönleinstrasse. The walk ends at the Rathaus Neukölln station.

South of Kreuzberg, northern Neukölln knows what it's like to go from troubled neighbourhood to hipster haven. For decades the area made headlines, mostly for its high crime rate and poor schools, only to get 'discovered' a few years ago by a cash-poor and idea-rich international crowd. Today the 'hood flaunts a thriving DIY ethos and teems with funky bars, galleries, project spaces and cafes, most of them run by a cast of creative neo-Berliners.

❶ Canalside Marketeering

Start by walking along the Maybachufer, a scenic section of the Landwehrkanal, ideally on Tuesday or Friday afternoons when the **Türkischer Markt** (Turkish Market; www.tuerkenmarkt.de; Maybachufer; ⏱11am-6.30pm Tue & Fri; Ⓤ Schönleinstrasse) is in full swing. Join hipsters in their quest for exotic cheesespreads, crusty flatbreads and mountains of produce.

❷ CafeShop

Is it a store? Or a cafe? In fact, **Sing Blackbird** (🕿030-5484 5051; www.facebook.com/singblackbird; Sanderstrasse 11; ⏱2-8pm; 🛜; Ⓤ Schönleinstrasse) sings its song for lovers of vintage clothing and fabulous homemade cakes and locally roasted java, all in one convenient spot.

❸ Frosty Delights

Ice-cream parlour **Fräulein Frost** (🕿030-9559 5521; Friedelstrasse 39; ⏱1pm-evening Mon-Fri, noon-evening Sat & Sun, closing time depends on weather; 🛜; Ⓤ Schönleinstrasse) is all about experimentation, as reflected in such courageous – and delectable – concoctions as apple-ginger or GuZiMi, which stands for Gurke-Zitrone-Minze (cucumber-lemon-mint).

❹ Burger Bonanza

The guys at **Berlin Burger International** (🕿0160 482 6505; www.berlinburgerinternational.com; Pannierstrasse 5; burgers €5-8.50; ⏱noon-midnight Mon-Thu, to 1am Fri, to 10pm Sun; 🍴; Ⓤ Hermannplatz) know that

size matters. At least when it comes to burgers: handmade, two-fisted, bulging and sloppy contenders.

❺ Weserstrasse Imbibing

This is the main drag to feed your party animal, with an eclectic mix of pubs and bars. Top picks include beers at **Ä** (🕿030-3064 8751; www.ae-neukoelln.de; Weserstrasse 40; ⏱5pm-late; 🚌M41, Ⓤ Rathaus Neukölln), wine at **Vin Aqua Vin** (🕿030-9405 2886; www.vinaquavin.de; Weserstrasse 204; ⏱4pm-midnight or later Mon-Wed, from 3pm Thu & Fri, from 2pm Sat; 🚌171, M29, M41, Ⓤ Hermannplatz) or cocktails at **Thelonius** (🕿030-5561 8232; www.facebook.com/theloniousbar berlin; Weserstrasse 202; ⏱7pm-2am or later; Ⓤ Hermannplatz).

❻ Nose to Tail

The folks behind foodie fave **Industry Standard** (🕿030-6272 7732; www.industrystandard.de; Sonnenallee 83; small plates €1.50-16; ⏱6-11pm Wed-Sun, 10am-3pm Sun; 🛜; 🚌M41, Ⓤ Rathaus Neukölln) serve even such perceived low-brow animal parts as tongue, heart or marrow in a most sophisticated fashion.

❼ Rooftop Chilling

During the warmer months, the clubgarden-bar combo **Klunkerkranich** (www.klunkerkranich.de; Karl-Marx-Strasse 66; ⏱10am-1.30am Mon-Sat, noon-1.30am Sun, weather permitting; 🛜; Ⓤ Rathaus Neukölln) is a fab place for day-drinking and chilling to local DJs or bands. It's up on the rooftop parking deck of the Neukölln Arcaden shopping mall.

Explore

Friedrichshain

Friedrichshain is famous for such high-profile GDR-era relics as the longest surviving stretch of Berlin Wall (the East Side Gallery), the socialist boulevard Karl-Marx-Allee and the former Stasi headquarters. But the area also stakes it reputation on having Berlin's most rambunctious nightlife scene with a glut of clubs and bars holding forth along Revaler Strasse and around the Ostkreuz train station.

The Sights in a Day

Make your way to Ostbahnhof and confront the ghosts of the Cold War on a stroll along the **East Side Gallery** (p120). After giving your camera a workout, enjoy Spree River views from the pretty **Oberbaumbrücke**, then enjoy coffee at **Cantina Universale** (p121) or pop into **Michelberger** (p124) for an early lunch.

Energies renewed, walk over to **Karl-Marx-Allee** (p124), former East Berlin's showcase boulevard, to parade alongside the phalanx of monumental buildings, some clad in Meissen tiles. Hop on the U5 at Strausberger Platz to ride the three stops to Samariterstrasse, then head towards Boxhagener Platz to embark on an aimless wander, poking into boho boutiques and watching the world on parade while chilling in a cafe.

Reflect upon the day's events over locally brewed pilsner at **Hops & Barley** (p126), then waltz over to **Lemon Leaf** (p124) for an Asian dinner or **Schneeweiss** (p124) for Alpine cuisine. Wrap up the evening over cocktails at **Chapel Bar** (p126) or find your fave from among the clubs and bars on the **RAW Gelände** (p126) along Revaler Strasse.

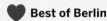

◉ Top Sights
East Side Gallery (p120)

♥ Best of Berlin

Clubs
Berghain/Panorama Bar (p125)

://about blank (p126)

Salon zur Wilden Renate (p126)

Gay & Lesbian
Himmelreich (p127)

Berghain/Panorama Bar (p125)

Shopping
Flohmarkt am Boxhagener Platz (p127)

Bars
Hops & Barley (p126)

Getting There

S S-Bahn Ostbahnhof is handy for the East Side Gallery; Warschauer Strasse and Ostkreuz for Boxhagener Platz and Revaler Strasse.

U U-Bahn The U1 links Warschauer Strasse with Kreuzberg, Schöneberg and Charlottenburg; the U5 runs east from Alexanderplatz down Karl-Marx-Allee and beyond.

🚋 Tram M10 links Warschauer Strasse with Prenzlauer Berg; M13 runs from Warschauer Strasse to Boxhagener Platz.

Top Sights
East Side Gallery

The year was 1989. After 28 years the Berlin Wall, that grim divider of humanity, met its maker. Most of it was quickly dismantled, but a 1.3km stretch along Mühlenstrasse, between Oberbaumbrücke and Ostbahnhof, became the East Side Gallery, the world's largest open-air mural strip. In more than 100 paintings, 129 artists from 20 countries translated the era's global euphoria and optimism into a mix of political statements, drug-induced musings and truly artistic visions. Today it's a memorial to the fall of the Wall and the peaceful reunification that followed.

👁 Map p122, C4

www.eastsidegallery-berlin.de

Mühlenstrasse btwn Oberbaumbrücke & Ostbahnhof

admission free

🕑 24hr

Ⓤ Warschauer Strasse,
Ⓢ Ostbahnhof, Warschauer Strasse

Street art, East Side Gallery

Don't Miss

Dimitry Vrubel: My God, Help Me Survive amid This Deadly Love

The gallery's best-known painting, showing Soviet and GDR leaders Leonid Brezhnev and Erich Honecker locking lips with eyes closed, is based on an actual photograph taken by French journalist Regis Bossu during Brezhnev's 1979 Berlin visit. This kind of kiss was an expression of great respect in socialist countries.

Birgt Kinder: Test the Rest

Another shutterbug favourite is Birgit Kinder's painting of a GDR-era Trabant car (known as a Trabi) bursting through the Wall with the licence plate reading 'NOV•9–89', the day the barrier was shattered.

Kani Alavi: It Happened in November

A wave of people squeezes through a breached Wall in a metaphorical rebirth in Kani Alavi's recollection of the events of 9 November. Note the different facial expressions, ranging from hope, joy and euphoria to disbelief and fear.

Thierry Noir: Homage to the Young Generation

French artist Thierry Noir's boldly coloured cartoon-like heads symbolise the new-found freedom after the Wall's collapse.

Thomas Klingenstein: Detour to the Japanese Sector

Born in East Berlin, Thomas Klingenstein spent time in a Stasi prison for dissent before being extradited to West Germany in 1980. This mural was inspired by his childhood love for Japan, where he ended up living from 1984 to the mid-'90s.

☑ Top Tips

▶ The more famous paintings are near the Ostbahnhof end, so start your walk here if you've got limited time.

▶ For more street art and graffiti, check out the river-facing side of the East Side Gallery.

▶ The grassy strip between the gallery and Spree River is a nice spot for chilling with a picnic or a cold beer. There are supermarkets in the Ostbahnhof.

✗ Take a Break

On weekdays, mingle with the Universal Music staff on the lovely riverside terrace of their **Cantina Universale** (www.universal-osthafen. de; Stralauer Allee 1; mains €5.50-7.50; ⏰8am-8pm Mon-Fri Apr-Sep, to 6pm Mon-Fri Oct-Mar; 🛜🍴; Ⓢ Warschauer Strasse, Ⓤ Warschauer Strasse).

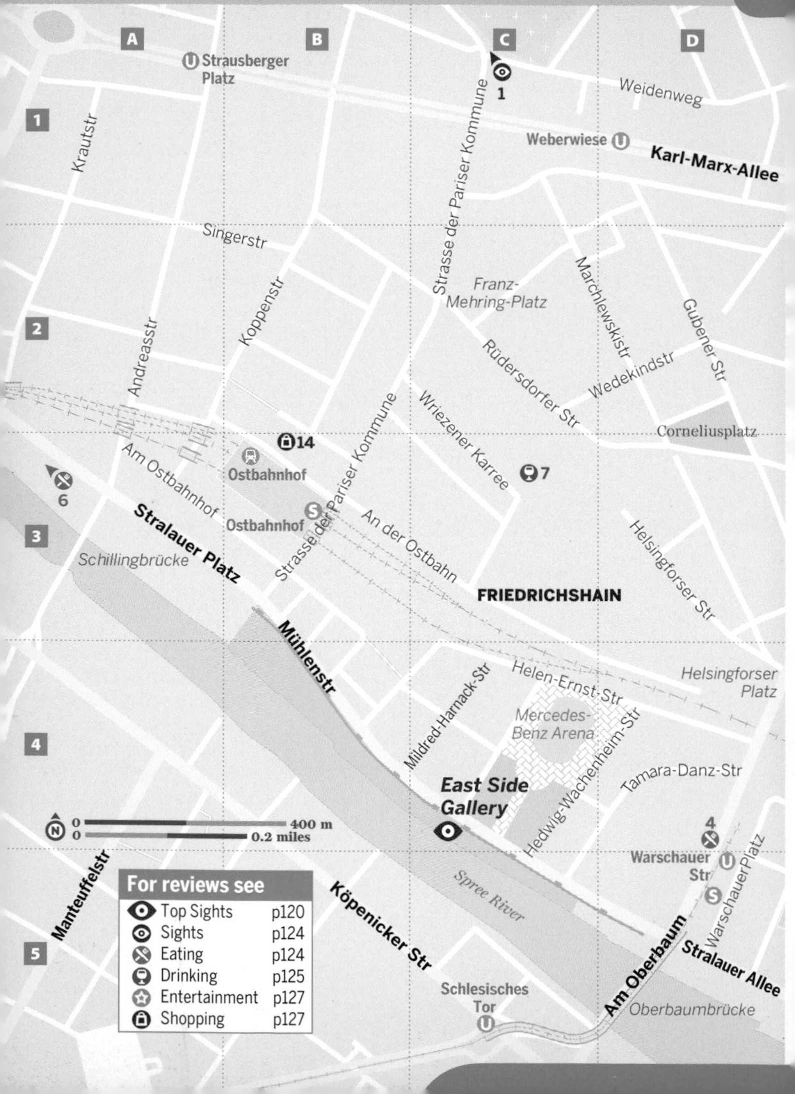

A B C D

1

Ⓤ Strausberger Platz

Weidenweg

Weberwiese Ⓤ

Karl-Marx-Allee

Krautstr

●1

Singerstr

Franz-Mehring-Platz

Strasse der Pariser Kommune

Marchlewskistr

Gubener Str

2

Andreasstr

Koppenstr

Rüdersdorfer Str

Wedekindstr

Wriezener Karree

Corneliusplatz

Am Ostbahnhof

🔒14

⊙ Ostbahnhof

●7

●6

Stralauer Platz

Ⓢ Ostbahnhof

An der Ostbahn

Helsingforser Str

3

Schillingbrücke

Strasse der Pariser Kommune

FRIEDRICHSHAIN

Mühlenstr

Helen-Ernst-Str

Helsingforser Platz

4

Mildred-Harnack-Str

Mercedes-Benz Arena

Hedwig-Wachenheim-Str

Tamara-Danz-Str

East Side Gallery
⊙

●4
✕
Warschauer Str Ⓤ

Warschauer Platz

Manteuffelstr

▲
Ⓝ
0 ─── 400 m
0 ─── 0.2 miles

Köpenicker Str

Spree River

Ⓢ

Am Oberbaum

Stralauer Allee

Schlesisches Tor Ⓤ

Oberbaumbrücke

For reviews see	
⊙ Top Sights	p120
⊙ Sights	p124
✕ Eating	p124
🍷 Drinking	p125
★ Entertainment	p127
🔒 Shopping	p127

5

Sights

Volkspark Friedrichshain PARK

1 Map p122, C1

Berlin's oldest public park has provided relief from urbanity since 1840, but has been hilly only since the late 1940s when wartime debris was piled up here to create two 'mountains' – the taller one, **Mont Klamott**, rises 78m high. Diversions include expansive lawns for lazing, tennis courts, a halfpipe for skaters, a couple of handily placed beer gardens and an outdoor cinema. (bounded by Am Friedrichshain, Friedenstrasse, Danziger Strasse & Landsberger Allee; P; 142, 200, M5, M6, M8, M10, USchillingstrasse)

Karl-Marx-Allee STREET

2 Map p122, E1

It's easy to feel like Gulliver in the Land of Brobdingnag when walking down monumental Karl-Marx-Allee, one of Berlin's most impressive GDR-era relics. Built between 1952 and 1960, the 90m-wide boulevard runs for 2.3km between Alexanderplatz and Frankfurter Tor and is a fabulous showcase of East German architecture. A considerable source of national pride back then, it provided modern flats for comrades and served as a backdrop for military parades. (admission free; UStrausberger Platz, Weberwiese, Frankfurter Tor)

Eating

Lemon Leaf ASIAN €€

3 Map p122, F3

Cheap, cheerful and stylish, this place is always swarmed by loyal locals, and for good reason: light, inventive and fresh, the South Asian menu has few false notes. Intriguing choice: the sweet-sour Indochine salad with banana blossoms. (030-2900 9428; www.lemonleaf.de; Grünberger Strasse 69; mains €8-14; noon-midnight; ; M10; UFrankfurter Tor)

Michelberger MEDITERRANEAN €€

4 Map p122, D4

Ensconced in one of Berlin's hippest hotels (p177), Michelberger makes mouthwatering Mediterranean-influenced dishes that often combine unusual organic ingredients in creative ways. Also a nice place for breakfast and a handy launch pad for a stroll along the East Side Gallery. (030-2977 8590; www.michelbergerhotel.com; Warschauer Strasse 39-40; mains lunch €8-10, dinner €12-23; 7-11am, noon-3pm & 7-11pm; ; SWarschauer Strasse, UWarschauer Strasse)

Schneeweiss GERMAN €€

5 Map p122, F3

The chilly-chic all-white decor with an eye-catching 'ice' chandelier hints at the Alpine menu at this fine-dining pioneer in Friedrichshain. Classics

SERGEY KELIN/SHUTTERSTOCK ©

Märchenbrunnen (Fairy Tale Fountain), Volkspark Friedrichshain

like schnitzel or cheese *spaetzle* to more innovative creations like braised pork belly with scallops all feature on the menu. Reservations essential for weekend brunch (10am to 4pm). (☎030-2904 9704; www.schneeweiss-berlin. de; Simplonstrasse 16; mains €11-18; ⊗noon-4pm Mon-Fri May-Oct, 6pm-1am Mon-Fri, 10am-1am Sat & Sun year-round; 👬; 🚃M13, Ⓤ Warschauer Strasse, Ⓢ Warschauer Strasse)

Fame Restaurant INTERNATIONAL €€

6 ✗ Map p122, A3

From the homemade bread to the wicked crème brûlée, dining at this carefully designed ramshackle space under the U-Bahn tracks is very much a Berlin experience. Run by the legendary Bar 25/Katerschmaus folks, Fame features meaty, fishy and vegetarian mains meant to be paired with a selection of seasonal side dishes. Reservations essential. (☎030-5105 2134; www.fame.katerschmaus.de; Holzmark-lstrasse 25; mains €12-21; ⊗noon-3pm Tue Fri, 7-11pm Tue-Sat; 🛜; Ⓤ Jannowitzbrücke, Ⓢ Jannowitzbrücke)

Drinking

Berghain/Panorama Bar CLUB

7 🍷 Map p122, C3

Only world-class spinmasters heat up this hedonistic bass-junkie hellhole inside a labyrinthine ex–power plant. Hard-edged minimal

 Local Life
Urban Playground
The jumble of derelict buildings called **RAW Gelände** (www.raw-tempel.de; along Revaler Strasse; **S** Warschauer Strasse, Ostkreuz, **U** Warschauer Strasse) is one of the last subcultural compounds in central Berlin. Founded in 1867 as a train repair station (Reichsbahn-Ausbesserungs-Werk, aka RAW), it remained in operation until 1994. Since 1999 the graffiti-slathered grounds have been a thriving offbeat sociocultural centre for creatives of all stripes. They also harbour clubs, bars, an indoor skate park, a swimming pool club and a bunker turned climbing wall. On Sundays, treasure hunters invade for the flea market.

techno dominates the ex–turbine hall (Berghain) while house dominates at Panorama Bar, one floor up. Strict door, no cameras. Check the website for midweek concerts and record-release parties at the main venue and the adjacent Kantine am Berghain. (www.berghain.de; Am Wriezener Bahnhof; ☺midnight Fri-Mon morning; **S** Ostbahnhof)

://about blank
CLUB

8 Map p122, G5

At this gritty multifloor party pen with lots of nooks and crannies, a steady line-up of top DJs feeds a diverse bunch of revellers danceworthy electronic gruel. Intense club nights usually segue into the morning

and beyond. Run by a collective, the venue also hosts cultural, political and gender events. (www.aboutparty.net; Markgrafendamm 24c; ☺hours vary, always Fri & Sat; **S** Ostkreuz)

Salon zur Wilden Renate
CLUB

9 Map p122, G5

Yes, things can indeed get pretty wild at Renate. Stellar local spinners feed self-ironic free-thinkers with sweat-inducing electro in the rambling rooms of an abandoned residential building. Sofas, a fireplace room and several bars provide suitable chill zones, as does the garden in summer. (☎030-2504 1426; www.renate.cc; Alt-Stralau 70; ☺hours vary, always from midnight Fri & Sat; **S** Ostkreuz)

Chapel Bar
COCKTAIL BAR

10 Map p122, G4

A star in the Friedrichshain cocktail firmament, the Chapel Bar has a delightfully cluttered look and a convivial vibe thanks to a crowd more interested in good drinks than looking good. The folks behind the bar wield the shaker with confidence, be it to create classics or their own 'liquid dreams' like the whisky-based Köppernickel. (☎0157 3200 0032; www.chapelberlin.com; Sonntagstrasse 30; ☺6pm-1am Sun-Wed, to 2am Thu, to 3.30am Fri & Sat; **S** Ostkreuz)

Hops & Barley
PUB

11 Map p122, F3

Conversation flows as freely as the unfiltered Pilsner, malty *Dunkel* (dark) and fruity *Weizen* (wheat) produced right here at one of Berlin's oldest craft breweries. The pub is inside a former butcher's shop and still has the tiled walls to prove it. Two projectors show football (soccer) games. (📞030-2936 7534; www.hopsandbarley-berlin.de; Wühlischstrasse 22/23; ⏰from 5pm Mon-Fri, from 3pm Sat & Sun; 🚋M13, Ⓤ Warschauer Strasse, Ⓢ Warschauer Strasse)

Himmelreich

GAY & LESBIAN

12 🚇 Map p122, F3

Confirming all those stereotypes about gay people having good taste, this candle-lit and pretence-free drinking cove makes most of the competition look like a straight guy's bedsit. Try the Prosit Beer, which is especially brewed for Himmelreich. (📞030-2936 9292; www.himmelreich-berlin.de; Simon-Dach-Strasse 36; ⏰6pm-2am or later Mon-Sat, 4pm-1am or later Sun; 🚋M13, Ⓢ Warschauer Strasse, Ⓤ Warschauer Strasse)

Entertainment

Astra Kulturhaus

LIVE MUSIC

13 ⭐ Map p122, E4

With space for 1500, easygoing Astra is one of the bigger indie venues in town, yet it often fills up easily, and not just when international headliners hit the stage. The party roster lures punters with electro swing, indie rock, techno and other sounds across the spectrum. Bonus: the gold-and-red colour scheme and sweet '50s East

Berlin decor vestiges. (📞030-2005 6767, tickets 030-6110 1313; www.astra-berlin. de; Revaler Strasse 99; ⏰hours vary, always Thu-Sat; 🚋M13, Ⓢ Warschauer Strasse, Ⓤ Warschauer Strasse)

Shopping

Antikmarkt am Ostbahnhof

ANTIQUES

14 🔒 Map p122, B3

If you're after antiques and collectibles, head to this sprawling market outside the Ostbahnhof station's north exit. The Grosser Antikmarkt (large antiques market) is more professional and brims with old coins, Iron Curtain–era relics, gramophone records, books, stamps, jewellery etc. It segues neatly into the Kleiner Antikmarkt (small antiques market), which has more bric-a-brac and lower prices. (Erich-Steinfurth-Strasse; ⏰9am-5pm Sun; Ⓢ Ostbahnhof)

Flohmarkt am Boxhagener Platz

MARKET

15 🔒 Map p122, F3

Wrapped around leafy Boxhagener Platz, this fun flea market is just a java whiff away from Sunday brunch cafes. It's easy to sniff out the pro vendors from the regular folks here to unload their spring-cleaning detritus. Usually a good selection of vinyl and books. (Boxhagener Platz; ⏰10am-6pm Sun; 🚋M13, Ⓢ Warschauer Strasse, Ⓤ Warschauer Strasse, Samariterstrasse)

Explore

Prenzlauer Berg

Prenzlauer Berg went from rags to riches after reunification, to emerge as one of Berlin's most desirable neighbourhoods. There are no must-sees, just ample local charms that reveal themselves on a leisurely meander. Look up at restored townhouses, comb side streets for indie boutiques or carve out a spot in a charismatic cafe. On Sundays, the Mauerpark is a haven of fun, flea-market browsing and karaoke.

Explore 129

The Sights in a Day

A great start to the day is the irresistible combo of strong coffee and a lazy breakfast at **Anna Blume** (p138), preferably at a sidewalk table. Spend the rest of the morning strolling down to **Kollwitzplatz** (p134), popping into indie boutiques for fashions, furnishings, baby clothing and other desirables. Walk north via leafy Husemannstrasse to the red-brick **Kulturbrauerei** (p134) and plunge into daily life in East Germany at the **Museum in der Kulturbrauerei** (p134).

Order a *Currywurst* (curried sausage) at **Konnopke's Imbiss** (p136), then put in a bit more shopping along Kastanienallee and Oderberger Strasse before heading over to the **Mauerpark** (p131) and trying to visualise what it looked like when the Berlin Wall ran through it.

Make your way back to Kastanienallee and stake out a table beneath the towering chestnuts of **Prater** (p137), Berlin's oldest beer garden. For dinner, consider **Umami** (p136) for light Vietnamese or perhaps authentic German rib stickers at **Zum Schusterjungen** (p137), followed by cocktails at **Bryk Bar** (p138).

For a local's day in Prenzlauer Berg, see p130.

Local Life

Sundays in the Mauerpark (p130)

Best of Berlin

Eating
Chutnify (p134)

Umami (p136)

Habba Habba (p135)

Konnopke's Imbiss (p136)

Lucky Leek (p137)

Bars
Prater Biergarten (p137)

Weinerei Forum (p137)

Becketts Kopf (p138)

Getting There

U-Bahn The U2 stops at Schönhauser Allee, Eberswalder Strasse and Senefelderplatz en route to Alexanderplatz, Gendarmenmarkt and western Berlin.

Tram The M1 links Museumsinsel and Prenzlauer Berg via the Scheunenviertel. The M13 goes straight into Friedrichshain party central.

S S-Bahn The main hub is Schönhauser Allee station (S8, S9, S41, S42).

JOHN FREEMAN/GETTY IMAGES ©

Local Life
Sundays in the Mauerpark

Locals, neo-Berliners and tourists – everyone flocks to the Mauerpark on Sundays. It's an energetic urban tapestry where a flea market, karaoke and bands provide entertainment, and people gather for barbecues, basketball and boules. A graffiti-covered section of the Berlin Wall recalls the time when the park was part of the death strip separating East and West Berlin.

❶ Coffee Deluxe

The pioneers of third-wave coffee in Berlin, **Bonanza Coffee Heroes** (www. bonanzacoffee.de; Oderberger Strasse 35; ⊘8.30am-6.30pm Mon-Fri, 10am-6.30pm Sat & Sun; 📶; 🚋M1, M10, 12, Ⓤ Eberswalder Strasse) make a mean cuppa java from freshly roasted top-flight beans in their tiny industrial-flavoured cafe. Lines can be long, giving you plenty of time to inhale the tempting aroma and to admire the hip laboratory-like

set up with its shiny machines, mills and filters.

② Confronting Cold War History

During the Cold War, East clashed against West at Bernauer Strasse, now paralleled by the 1.4km-long **Gedenkstätte Berliner Mauer** (p74), a multimedia memorial that illustrates the realities of life with the Berlin Wall. Even exploring just a short stretch of it is an eye-opening experience.

③ Urban Archaeology

After this dose of history, hit the **Flohmarkt am Mauerpark** (www.flohmarktimmauerpark.de; Bernauer Strasse 63-64; ⊙9am-6pm Sun; 🚊M1, M10, 12, ⓊEberswalder Strasse) for some quality hunting and gathering of retro threads, cool stuff by local designers, GDR-era household items and vintage vinyl. Afterwards, fortify yourself at a street-food stall or drag your loot to a market beer garden and chill out in the sun.

④ Bearpit Karaoke

On most summer Sundays, Berlin's best free entertainment kicks off around 3pm when Joe Hatchiban sets up his custom-made mobile karaoke unit in the Mauerpark's amphitheatre. As many as 2000 people cram on to the stone bleachers to cheer and clap for eager crooners ranging from giggling 11-year-olds to Broadway-calibre belters. Confirm dates on Facebook.

⑤ Falkplatz

Studded with ancient chestnut, oak, birch, ash and poplar trees, this leafy park was a parade ground for Prussian soldiers back in the 19th century. Today, it's a great place to relax on the grass and watch kids frolicking around the sea-lion fountain.

⑥ Burgermania

New York meets Berlin at expat favourite **Bird** (📞030-5105 3283; www.thebirdinberlin.com; Am Falkplatz 5; burgers €9.50-14, steaks from €22.50; ⊙6pm-midnight Mon-Thu, 4pm-midnight Fri, noon-midnight Sat & Sun; 🔊; 🚊M1, ⓊSchönhauser Allee, ⓈSchönhauser Allee), whose dry-aged steaks, burgers and hand-cut fries might just justify the hype. Sink your teeth into a dripping half-pounder made from freshly ground premium German beef trapped between a toasted English muffin (yes, it's messy – that's what the kitchen roll is for!).

⑦ Northern Mauerpark

To escape the Mauerpark frenzy and see where the locals relax, head north of the Gleimstrasse tunnel. This is where you'll find an enchanting birch grove, an educational farm playground and the 'Schwedter North Face' climbing wall operated by the German Alpine Club.

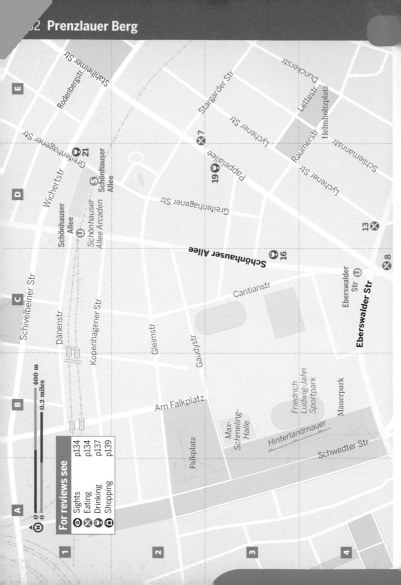

For reviews see

◎	Sights	p134
✕	Eating	p134
✕	Drinking	p137
🛍	Shopping	p139

0 400 m
0 0.2 miles

Danziger Str

17 🅿

Christburger Str

Rykestr

22 🅂
Marienburger Str

Prenzlauer Allee

5 🅧
18 🅿

Husemannstr

Sredzkistr

10 🅧

Knaackstr

Kollwitzplatz
4 🅾

Belforter Str

Strassburger Str

Museum in der
Kulturbrauerei
2 🅾

12 🅧

Wörther Str

Kollwitzstr

Metzer Str

Saarbrücker Str

1 🅾
Kulturbrauerei

Schönhauser Allee

3 🅾
Jüdischer Friedhof
Schönhauser Allee

Schwedter Str

Senefelderplatz Ⓤ

20 Ⓤ

Schönhauser Allee

15 🅿

PRENZLAUER
BERG

6 🅧

Oderberger Str

11 🅧

Teutoburger
Platz

24 🅾

Kastanienallee

Choriner Str

Fehrbelliner Str

Chorinier Str

Schwedter Str

Bernauer Str

9 🅧

Weinbergsweg

Zionskirchplatz

Arkonaplatz
23 🅾

Ruppinerstr

14 🅿

Volkspark am
Weinbergsweg

Fehrbelliner Str

Veteranenstr

Rosenthaler
Platz Ⓤ

Torstr

Brunnenstr

5

6

7

8

E

D

C

B

A

Sights

Kulturbrauerei
HISTORIC BUILDING

1 Map p132, C5

The fanciful red-and-yellow brick buildings of this 19th-century brewery have been recycled into a cultural powerhouse with a small village's worth of venues, from concert and theatre halls to nightclubs, shops, a multiplex cinema and a free GDR history museum. From spring to fall, foodies invade for the Sunday street-food market. (☏030-4431 5152; www.kulturbrauerei.de; btwn Schönhauser Allee, Knaackstrasse, Eberswalder Strasse & Sredzskistrasse; ⌖M1, Ⓤ Eberswalder Strasse)

Museum in der Kulturbrauerei
MUSEUM

2 Map p132, D5

This exhibit uses original documents and objects (including a camper-style Trabi car) to teach the rest of us about daily life in East Germany. Four themed sections juxtapose the lofty aspirations of the socialist state with the sobering realities of material shortages, surveillance and oppression. Case studies show the different paths individuals took to deal with their living conditions. (☏030-467 777 911; www.hdg.de; Knaackstrasse 97; admission free; ⌖10am-6pm Tue, Wed & Fri-Sun, to 8pm Thu; ⌖M1, 12, Ⓤ Eberswalder Strasse)

Jüdischer Friedhof Schönhauser Allee
CEMETERY

3 Map p132, C7

Berlin's second Jewish cemetery opened in 1827 and hosts many well-known dearly departed, such as the artist Max Liebermann. It's a pretty place with dappled light filtering through big old trees and a sense of melancholy emanating from overgrown graves and toppled tombstones. The nicest and oldest have been moved to the Lapidarium by the main entrance. (☏030-441 9824; www.jg-berlin.org; Schönhauser Allee 23-25; ⌖8am-4pm Mon-Thu, 7.30am-2.30pm Fri; Ⓤ Senefelderplatz)

Kollwitzplatz
SQUARE

4 Map p132, D6

Triangular Kollwitzplatz is the epicentre of Prenzlauer Berg gentrification. To pick up on the local vibe, linger with macchiato mamas and media daddies in a street cafe or join them at the **farmers market** (Kollwitzstrasse; ⌖noon-7pm Thu, 9am-4pm Sat). The park in the square's centre is tot heaven with three playgrounds plus a bronze sculpture of the artist Käthe Kollwitz for clambering on. (⌖; Ⓤ Senefelderplatz)

Eating

Chutnify
INDIAN €

5 Map p132, E5

Aparna Aurora's little restaurant is spicing up Berlin's rather bland Indian food scene. Here the focus is on au-

Kulturbrauerei

thentic South Indian street food with a special nod to dosas (a type of crêpe) filled with everything from potato masala to tandoori chicken. (✆030-4401 0795; www.chutnify.com; Sredzkistrasse 43; mains €6.50-8.50; ⊘noon-11pm Tue-Sun; ✈; ⊜M2, M10, Ⓤ Eberswalder Strasse)

Habba Habba MIDDLE EASTERN €

 6 Map p132, C5

This tiny *Imbiss* (snack bar) makes the best wraps in town for our money, especially the one stuffed with tangy pomegranate-marinated chicken and nutty buckwheat dressed in a minty yoghurt sauce. Other faves include the halloumi salad and the coriander kofta. All dishes are available in vege-

tarian and vegan versions. (✆030-3674 5726; www.habba-habba.de; Kastanienallee 15; dishes €4.50-9; ⊘10am-10pm; ✈; ⊜M1, 12, Ⓤ Eberswalder Strasse)

Zia Maria ITALIAN €

 7 Map p132, E2

This pizza kitchen cum gallery gets a big thumbs up for its freshly made crispy-crust pies with classic and eclectic toppings, including wafer-thin prosciutto, nutmeg-laced artichokes and pungent Italian sausage. Two slices are enough to fill up most bellies. Pour your own wine from the barrel. (www.pizzaziamaria.de; Pappelallee 32a; pizza slices €1.50-3.50; ⊘noon-11.30pm; ⊜12, Ⓢ Schönhauser Allee, Ⓤ Schönhauser Allee)

Local Life
Knaackstrasse Cafe Scene

Mere steps from Kollwitzplatz, pretty Knaackstrasse is a quiet residential street with a row of charming cafes and restaurants perfect for people-watching while enjoying breakfast or a beer at a sunny sidewalk table. The round tower opposite is Berlin's oldest water tower (1877), now honeycombed with pie-sliced flats. In Nazi Germany, its machine room went through a sinister stint as an improvised prison and torture centre.

Konnopke's Imbiss GERMAN €

 8 Map p132, C4

Brave the inevitable queue at this famous sausage kitchen, ensconced in the same spot below the elevated U-Bahn tracks since 1930, but now equipped with a heated pavilion and an English menu. The 'secret' sauce topping its classic *Currywurst* comes in a four-tier heat scale from mild to wild. (☎030-442 7765; www.konnopke-imbiss.de; Schönhauser Allee 44a; sausages €1.30-2; ⏰9am-8pm Mon-Fri, 11.30am-8pm Sat; ☒M1, M10, ⓤEberswalder Strasse)

W-Der Imbiss FUSION €

 9 Map p132, B7

The self-described home of 'indo-mexical-ital' fusion, W has for years been delighting fans with its signature naan pizza freshly baked in the tandoor oven and decorated with anything from avocado to smoked salmon. The fish tacos, thali curry spread and tandoori salmon also have their fans. (☎030-4435 2206; www.w-derimbiss.de; Kastanienallee 49; dishes €5-12; ⏰noon-10pm Sun-Thu, to 11pm Fri & Sat; ☒; ☒M1, ⓤRosenthaler Platz)

Umami VIETNAMESE €€

10 Map p132, E7

A mellow 1950s lounge-vibe and an inspired menu of Indochine home cooking divided into 'regular' and 'vegetarian' choices are the main draws of this restaurant with large pavement terrace. Leave room for the green-tea apple pie or a Vietnamese cupcake called 'popcake'. The six-course family meal is a steal at €20 (€9 per additional person). (☎030-2886 0626; www.umami-restaurant.de; Knaackstrasse 16-18; mains €7.50-15; ⏰noon-11.30pm; ☎☒; ☒M2, ⓤSenefelderplatz)

Standard – Serious Pizza ITALIAN €€

11 Map p132, C7

The name is definitely not the game, for the Neapolitan-style pizzas here are anything but standard. Topped with such quality ingredients as San Marzano tomatoes, from the heel of Vesuvius, they are tickled to perfection in a ferociously hot cupola furnace. (☎030-4862 5614; www.standard-berlin.de; Templiner Strasse 7; pizza €8.50-12.50; ⏰6pm-midnight Tue-Fri, 1pm-midnight Sat & Sun; ☎; ⓤSenefelderplatz)

Lucky Leek VEGAN €€

12 Map p132, D7

Josita Hartanto has a knack for coaxing maximum flavour out of the vegetable kingdom and for boldly combining ingredients in unexpected ways. Hers is one of the best vegan restaurants in town and is especially lovely in the summer, when seating expands to a leafy pavement terrace. No à la carte on Fridays and Saturdays. (☑030-6640 8710; www.lucky-leek.de; Kollwitzstrasse 54; mains €14-20, 3-/5-course dinners €33/55; ☉6-10pm Wed-Sun; ☑; Ⓤ Senefelderplatz)

Zum Schusterjungen GERMAN €€

13 Map p132, D4

At this old-school gastropub, rustic Berlin charm is doled out with as much abandon as the delish home cooking. Big platters of goulash, roast pork and sauerbraten feed both tummy and soul, as do the regionally brewed Berliner Schusterjunge Pilsner and Märkischer Landmann black beer. (☑030-442 7654; www.zumschusterjun-gen.com; Danziger Strasse 9; mains €9-17; ☉11am-midnight; Ⓤ Eberswalder Strasse)

Drinking

Weinerei Forum WINE BAR

14 Map p132, A7

After 8pm, this living-room-style cafe turns into a wine bar that works on the honour principle: you 'rent' a wine glass for €2, then help yourself to as much vino as you like and in the end decide what you want to pay. Please be fair to keep this fantastic concept going. (☑030-440 6983; www.weinerei. com; Fehrbelliner Strasse 57; ☉10am-midnight; 🛜; Ⓜ M1, Ⓤ Rosenthaler Platz)

Prater Biergarten BEER GARDEN

15 Map p132, C5

Berlin's oldest beer garden has seen beer-soaked nights since 1837 and is still a charismatic spot for guzzling a custom-brewed Prater Pilsner beneath the ancient chestnut trees (self-service). Kids can romp around the small play area. (☑030-448 5688; www. pratergarten.de; Kastanienallee 7-9; snacks €2.50-6; ☉noon-late Apr-Sep, weather permitting; Ⓤ Eberswalder Strasse)

Zum Starken August PUB

16 Map p132, C3

Part circus, part burlesque bar, this vibrant venue dressed in Victorian-era exuberance is a fun and friendly addition to the Prenzlauer Berg pub culture. Join the unpretentious, international crowd over cocktails and craft beers while being entertained with drag-hosted bingo, burlesque divas, wicked cabaret or the hilarious 'porno karaoke'. (☑030-2520 9020; www. zumstarkenaugust.de; Schönhauser Allee 56; ☉11am-1am Sun & Mon, to 2am Tue, to 3am Wed, to 4am Thu, to 5am Fri & Sat; Ⓜ M1, M10, Ⓤ Eberswalder Strasse)

ULLSTEIN BILD/CONTRIBUTOR/GETTY IMAGES ©

Stalls at Trödelmarkt Arkonaplatz

Bryk Bar
COCKTAIL BAR

17 Map p132, E5

Both vintage and industrial elements contribute to the unhurried, dapper ambience at this darkly lit cocktail lab. Bar chef Frank Grosser whips unusual ingredients into such experimental liquid teasers as Kamasutra with a Hangover, which blends rum with lemon, honey and a white chocolate and horseradish foam. (☏030-3810 0165; www.bryk-bar.com; Rykestrasse 18; ⊗noon-2am Sun-Thu, to 3am Fri & Sat; ☐M2, M10, Ⓢ Prenzlauer Allee)

Anna Blume
CAFE

18 Map p132, E5

Potent java, homemade cakes, and flowers from the attached shop perfume the art nouveau interior of this corner cafe named for a 1919 Dadaist poem by German artist Kurt Schwitters. In fine weather the outdoor terrace offers primo people watching. Great for breakfast (served any time), especially if you order the tiered tray for two. (☏030-4404 8749; www.cafe-anna-blume.de; Kollwitzstrasse 83; ⊗8am-midnight; ☐M2, M10, Ⓤ Eberswalder Strasse)

Becketts Kopf
COCKTAIL BAR

19 Map p132, D3

Past Samuel Beckett's portrait, the art of cocktail-making is taken very seriously. Settle into a heavy armchair in the warmly lit lounge and take your sweet time perusing the extensive – and poetic – drinks menu. All the classics are accounted for, of course, but it's the seasonal special concoctions that truly stimulate the senses. (☏030-9900 5188; www.becketts-kopf.de; Pappelallee 64; ⊗8pm-late; ☐12, Ⓢ Schönhauser Allee, Ⓤ Schönhauser Allee)

Bassy
CLUB

20 Map p132, C8

Most punters here have a post-Woodstock birthdate, but happily ride the retro wave at this trashy-charming concert and party den dedicated 'strictly' to pre-1969 sounds on vinyl – surf music, rockabilly, swing and country among them. Concerts, burlesque cabaret and the infamous Chantals House of Shame gay party on Thursdays beef up the schedule. Dress creatively... (📞030-3744 8020; www.bassy-club.de; Schönhauser Allee 176a; ⏰9pm-late, concerts 11pm; Ⓤ Senefelderplatz)

Greifbar
GAY

21 Map p132, D1

Men-Drinks-Cruising: Greifbar's motto says it all. (📞030-8975 1498; www.greifbar.com; Wichertstrasse 10; ⏰10pm-6am; Ⓢ Schönhauser Allee, Ⓤ Schönhauser Allee)

Shopping

Saint Georges
BOOKS

22 🔒 Map p132, E6

Laid-back and low-key, Saint Georges bookshop is a sterling spot to track down new and used English-language fiction and nonfiction. The selection includes plenty of rare and out-of-print books as well as literature by foreign authors translated into English. (📞030-8179 8333; www.saintgeorgesbookshop.com; Wörther Strasse 27; ⏰11am-8pm Mon-Fri, to 7pm Sat; 📶; Ⓤ Senefelderplatz)

Trödelmarkt Arkonaplatz
MARKET

23 🔒 Map p132, A6

Surrounded by cafes perfect for carbo-loading, this smallish flea market on

Top Tip

Shopping Areas

Prenzlauer Berg is mercifully devoid of chains. Streets where indie boutiques thrive include Kastanienallee, Stargarder Strasse, part of Schönhauser Allee, and the streets around Helmholtzplatz and Kollwitzplatz. Most shops don't open until 11am or later and close around 6pm or 7pm.

a leafy square lets you ride the retro frenzy with plenty of groovy furniture, accessories, clothing, vinyl and books, including some East German vintage items. It's easily combined with a visit to the nearby Flohmarkt im Mauerpark (p131). (www.troedelmarkt-arkonaplatz.de; Arkonaplatz; ⏰10am-4pm Sun; 🚋M1, M10, Ⓤ Bernauer Strasse)

VEB Orange
GIFTS & SOUVENIRS

24 🔒 Map p132, B5

Viva vintage! With its selection of the most beautiful things from the '60s and '70s (especially from East Germany), this place is a tangible reminder of how colourful, campy and fun home decor used to be. True to its name, many of the furnishings, accessories, lamps and fashions are orange in colour. (📞030-9788 6886; www.veb orange.de; Oderberger Strasse 29; ⏰11am-7pm Mon-Sat; Ⓤ Eberswalder Strasse)

Top Sights
Schloss & Park Sanssouci

Getting There

Potsdam is 24km southwest of the city centre.

Train It's 25 minutes from Berlin Hauptbahnhof or Zoologischer Garten to Potsdam Hauptbahnhof.

S-Bahn The S7 takes 40 minutes.

This glorious park-and-palace ensemble is what happens when a king has good taste, plenty and access to the finest architects and artists day. Sanssouci was dreamed up by Frederick Great (1712–86) and is anchored by the epony palace, built as a summer retreat in Potsdam quick train ride from Berlin. His great-great- Friedrich Wilhelm IV (1795–1861) added a few buildings. Unesco gave the entire complex Heritage status in 1990.

Sculpture in Park Sanssouci

Don't Miss

Schloss Sanssouci

The biggest stunner, and what everyone comes to see, is **Schloss Sanssouci** (adult/concession incl tour or audioguide €12/8; ☺10am-6pm Tue-Sun Apr-Oct, to 5pm Nov-Mar), Frederick the Great's famous summer palace. Designed by Georg Wenzeslaus von Knobelsdorff in 1747, the rococo gem sits daintily above vine-draped terraces with the king's grave nearby.

Standouts on the tours (guided or self-guided) include the **Konzertsaal** (Concert Hall), whimsically decorated with vines, grapes and even a cobweb where sculpted spiders frolic. Also note the intimate **Bibliothek** (library), lidded by a gilded sunburst ceiling, where the king would seek solace amid 2000 leather-bound tomes ranging from Greek poetry to the latest releases by his friend Voltaire. Another highlight is the **Marmorsaal** (Marble Room), an elegant white Carrara marble symphony modelled after the Pantheon in Rome.

Chinesisches Haus

The adorable **Chinese House** (adult/concession €3/2; ☺10am-6pm Tue-Sun May-Oct) is a shutterbug favourite thanks to an enchanting exterior of exotically dressed gilded figures sipping tea, dancing and playing musical instruments. Inside is a precious porcelain collection.

Bildergalerie

The **Picture Gallery** (adult/concession €6/5; ☺10am-6pm Tue-Sun May-Oct) shelters Frederick the Great's prized collection of Old Masters, including such pearls as Caravaggio's *Doubting Thomas,* Anthony van Dyck's *Pentecost* and several works by Peter Paul Rubens. Behind the rather plain facade hides a sumptuous symphony of gilded ornamentation, yellow and white marble and a patterned stone floor that is perhaps just as impressive as the mostly large-scale paintings.

☎0331-969 4200

www.spsg.de

Maulbeerallee

day passes adult/concession €19/14

☺varies

🚌606, 695 from Potsdam Hauptbahnhof

☑ Top Tips

▶ Book your timed ticket to Schloss Sanssouci online to avoid wait times and/or disappointment.

▶ Avoid visiting on Monday when most palaces are closed.

▶ Ticket sanssouci+, a one-day pass to palaces in Potsdam, costs €19 (concession €14) and is sold online and at each building.

✕ Take a Break

For international favourites, head to **Potsdam Zur Historischen Mühle** (☎0331-281 493; www.moevenpick-restaurants.com; Zur Historischen Mühle 2; mains €11.50-25; ☺8am-10pm; P🏋) with beer garden and children's playground.

Neues Palais

The final palace commissioned by Frederick the Great, the **Neues Palais** (adult/concession incl tour or audioguide €8/6; ☉10am-6pm Wed-Mon Apr-Oct, to 5pm Nov-Mar) has made-to-impress dimensions, a central dome and a lavish exterior capped with a parade of sandstone figures. After extensive restoration, most of the building highlights are once again accessible, including the shimmering festival hall called **Grottensaal** (Grotto Hall) and the magnificent **Marmorsaal** (Marble Hall). Also looking splendid is the redone **Unteres Fürstenquartie**r (Lower Royal Suite), which consists of a concert room, an oval-shaped chamber, an antechamber and, most impressively, a dining room with walls sheathed in red silk damask with gold-braided trim.

Orangerieschloss

Modelled after an Italian Renaissance villa, the 300m-long, 1864-built **Orangery Palace** (adult/concession €4/3; ☉10am-6pm Tue-Sun May-Oct, Sat & Sun Apr) was the favourite building project of Friedrich Wilhelm IV – a passionate Italophile. Its highlight is the **Raffaelsaal** (Raphael Hall), which brims with 19th-century copies of the famous painter's masterpieces.

Belvedere auf dem Klausberg

Frederick the Great's final building project was this temple-like **belvedere** (An der Orangerie 1; ☉open for special events only), modelled on Nero's palace in

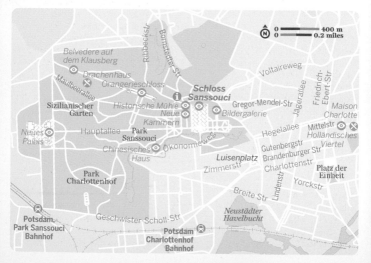

Rome. The panorama of park, lakes and Potsdam is predictably fabulous from up here. The upstairs hall has an impressive frescoed dome, oak parquet and fanciful stucco marble but, alas, it can be seen during special events only.

Neue Kammern

The **New Chambers** (adult/concession incl tour or audioguide €6/5; ⏱10am-6pm Tue-Sun Apr-Oct), built by Knobelsdorff in 1748, were originally an orangery and later converted into a guest palace. The interior drips with rococo opulence, most notably the square **Jasper Hall**, which is drenched in precious stones and lidded by a Venus fresco, and the **Ovidsaal**, a grand ballroom with gilded wall reliefs depicting scenes from *Metamorphosis*.

Park Charlottenhof

Laid out by Peter Lenńe for Friedrich Wilhelm IV, this park segues from Park Sanssouci but gets much fewer visitors. Buildings in this quiet corner bear the stamp of Karl Friedrich Schinkel, most notably the neoclassical **Schloss Charlottenhof** (Geschwister-Scholl-Strasse 34a; tours adult/concession €6/5; ⏱tours 10am-6pm Tue-Sun May-Oct), modelled after a Roman villa, and the nearby **Roman Baths** (adult/concession €5/4; ⏱10am-6pm Tue-Sun May-Oct), a picturesque ensemble of Italian country villas.

Historische Mühle

This reconstructed 18th-century Dutch-style **windmill** (Maulbeerallee 5; adult/concession €3/2; ⏱10am-6pm daily Apr-Oct, to 4pm Sat & Sun Nov & Jan-Mar)

Neue Kammern and the Historische Mühle

contains exhibits about the history of the mill and mill technology, and offers a close-up of the grinding mechanism and a top-floor viewing platform.

Nearby: Holländisches Viertel

To get a sense of Potsdam beyond the palaces, head east for about 1km via the pedestrianised Brandenburger Strasse shopping lane to the **Dutch Quarter** (www.hollaendisches-viertel.net; Mittelstrasse; 🚌606, 631), a picturesque cluster of 134 gabled red-brick houses built around 1730 for Dutch workers invited to Potsdam by Friedrich Wilhelm I. The pint-size quarter has been done up beautifully and brims with galleries, cafes and restaurants. Mittelstrasse is especially scenic.

STIFTUNG PREUSSISCHE SCHLOSSER UND GARTEN BERLIN BRANDENBURG/HANS BACH ©

The Best of
Berlin

Berlin's Best Walks

Berlin's Best...

Alfresco diners in Mitte
MAREMAGNUM/GETTY IMAGES ©

Best Walks
Historical Highlights

🏃 The Walk

This walk checks off Berlin's blockbuster landmarks as it cuts right through the historic city centre, Mitte (literally 'Middle'). This is the birthplace and glamorous heart of Berlin, a high-octane cocktail of culture, architecture and commerce. You'll follow in the footsteps of kings and soldiers, marvel at grand architecture and stroll cobbled lanes, travel from the Middle Ages to the future and be awed by some of the world's finest works of art. Bring that camera!

Start Reichstag; Ⓤ Bundestag, 🚌 100, TXL

Finish Nikolaiviertel; Ⓢ Alexanderplatz, Ⓤ Alexanderplatz

Length 3.5km; three hours

🍴 Take a Break

Cafe Einstein (📞 030-204 3632; www.einsteinudl.de; Unter den Linden 42; mains €12.50-16.50; ⏰ 7am-10pm) makes for an arty pit stop.

Nikolaiviertel

DANIEL VINE PHOTOGRAPHY/GETTY IMAGES ©

❶ Reichstag

The 1894 **Reichstag** (p24) is the historic anchor of Berlin's federal government quarter. The sparkling glass dome, added during the building's 1990s revamp, has become a shining beacon of unified Berlin.

❷ Brandenburg Gate

The only remaining gate of Berlin's 18th-century town wall, the **Brandenburg Gate** (p26) became an involuntary neighbour of the Berlin Wall during the Cold War. It's now a cheery symbol of German reunification.

❸ Unter den Linden

Originally a riding path linking the city palace with the royal hunting grounds in Tiergarten, **Unter den Linden** has been Berlin's showpiece road since the 18th century but is partly torn up thanks to the construction of a new U-Bahn line.

4 Gendarmenmarkt

Berlin's most beautiful square, **Gendarmenmarkt** (p32) is bookended by domed cathedrals with the famous Konzerthaus (Concert Hall) in between. The surrounding streets are lined with elegant hotels, restaurants and cocktail bars.

5 Museum Island

The sculpture-studded Palace Bridge leads to the twee Spree island whose northern half, **Museumsinsel**, is a Unesco-recognised treasure chest of art, sculpture and objects spread across five grand museums.

6 Humboldt Forum

Under construction opposite Museum Island is a replica of the old Prussian royal city palace that will house an art and cultural centre called the Humboldt Forum. For a primer, visit the **Humboldt-Box** (p49).

7 Berliner Dom

Pompous and majestic inside and out, the **Berlin Cathedral** (p49) is a symbol of Prussian imperial power and blessed with artistic treasures, royal sarcophagi and nice views from the gallery.

8 Nikolaiviertel

With its cobbled lanes and higgledy-piggledy houses, the **Nikolai Quarter** may look medieval but was actually built to celebrate Berlin's 750th birthday in 1987.

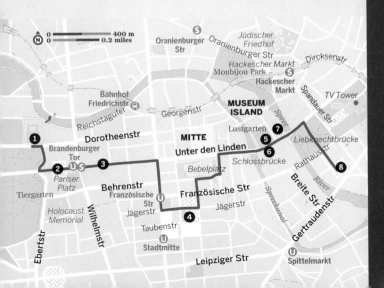

![runner icon] Best Walks
Walking the Wall

![walk icon] The Walk

Construction of the Berlin Wall began shortly after midnight on 13 August 1961. For the next 28 years this grim barrier divided a city and its people, becoming the most visible symbol of the Cold War. By now the city's halves have visually merged so perfectly that it takes a keen eye to tell East from West. To give you a sense of the period of division, this walk follows the most central section of the Berlin Wall. Along the way, information panels provide background and context in four languages.

Start Checkpoint Charlie; Ⓤ Kochstrasse

Finish Parlament der Bäume; Ⓤ Bundestag

Length 3km; two hours

![fork icon] Take a Break

Potsdamer Platz has the biggest concentration of eating and drinking options.

Watchtower, near Potsdamer Platz

WESTEND61 PREMIUM/SHUTTERSTOCK ©

❶ Checkpoint Charlie

As the third Allied checkpoint, **Checkpoint Charlie** (p65) got its name from the third letter in the NATO phonetic alphabet. Weeks after the Wall was built, US and Soviet tanks faced off here in one of the tensest moments of the Cold War.

❷ Niederkirchner Strasse

Along Niederkirchner Strasse looms a 200m-long section of the original **outer border wall**. Scarred by souvenir hunters, it's now protected by a fence. The border strip was very narrow here, with the inner wall abutting such buildings as the former Nazi Air Force Ministry.

❸ Watchtower

This mushroom-shaped structure is one of the few remaining **watchtowers**. Guards had to climb up a slim round shaft to reach the octagonal observation perch. Introduced in 1969, this cramped model was later replaced by larger square towers.

❹ Potsdamer Platz

Potsdamer Platz used to be a massive no-man's land bisected by the Wall and a 'death strip' several hundred metres wide. Outside the northern S-Bahn station entrance are a few **Berlin Wall segments**.

❺ Brandenburg Gate

The **Brandenburg Gate** (p26) was where construction of the Wall began. Many heads of state gave speeches in front of it, including former US president Ronald Reagan who, in 1987, uttered the famous words: 'Mr Gorbachev – tear down this wall!'

❻ Art Installations

In the basement of the Marie-Elisabeth-Lüders Haus, an **art installation** by Ben Wagin runs along the original course of the Berlin Wall. It consists of original segments, each painted with a year and the number of people killed at the Wall in that year. Enter from the Spree Promenade. If it's closed, you can easily sneak a peak through the window of this government building that houses the parliamentary library.

❼ Parlament der Bäume

Wagin also masterminded the **Parliament of Trees**, a quiet garden and environmental art installation. It consists not only of trees but of memorial stones, pictures, text and 58 original pieces of the Wall inscribed with the names of 258 victims.

Best Walks
A Leisurely Tiergarten Stroll

🏃 The Walk

Berlin's rulers used to hunt boar and pheasants in the rambling Tiergarten until garden architect Peter Lenné landscaped the grounds in the 18th century. Today it's one of the world's largest urban parks, popular for strolling, jogging, picnicking, Frisbee tossing and, yes, nude sunbathing.

Start Brandenburg Gate; S Brandenburger Tor, U Brandenburger Tor

Finish Potsdamer Platz; S Potsdamer Platz, U Potsdamer Platz

Length 4km; 1½ to two hours

🍴 Take a Break

At the lakeside beer garden **Cafe am Neuen See** (☎030-254 4930; www.cafeamneuensee.de; Lichtenstein-allee 2; ⏱restaurant 9am-11pm, beer garden 11am-late Mon-Fri, 10am-late Sat & Sun; 🚻; 🚌200, UZoologischer Garten, SZoologischer Garten, Tiergarten), cold beers go well with bratwurst, pretzels and pizza.

Sowjetisches Ehrenmal

① Strasse des 17 Juni

The broad boulevard bisecting Tiergarten was named **Street of 17 June** in honour of the victims of the bloodily quashed 1953 workers' uprising in East Berlin. Back in the 16th century, the road linked two royal palaces; it was doubled in width and turned into a triumphal road under Hitler.

② Sowjetisches Ehrenmal

The **Soviet War Memorial** is flanked by two Russian T-34 tanks said to have been the first to enter the city in 1945. It was built by German workers on order of the Soviets and completed just months after the end of the war. More than 2000 Red Army soldiers are buried behind the colonnade.

③ Schloss Bellevue

A succession of German presidents have made their home in snowy-white **Bellevue Palace**. The neoclassical pile was originally a pad for the youngest brother of King Frederick the Great, then became a school under Kaiser Wilhelm II and a museum of ethnology under the Nazis. It's closed to the public.

4 Siegessäule

Engulfed by roundabout traffic, the 1873 **Victory Column** was erected to celebrate Prussian military victories and is now a prominent symbol of Berlin's gay community. The gilded woman on top represents the goddess of

victory and is featured prominently in the Wim Wenders movie *Wings of Desire*. Climb to the top to appreciate the park's dimensions.

5 Rousseauinsel

One of Tiergarten's most idyllic spots is the **Rousseauinsel**, a teensy island in a placid pond that's a memorial to 18th-century French philosopher Jean-Jacques Rousseau. It was designed to resemble his actual burial site on an island

near Paris. Look for the stone pillar.

6 Luiseninsel

Another enchanting place, **Luiseninsel** is a tranquil gated garden brimming with statues and redolent with seasonal flower beds. It was created after Napoleon's occupying troops left town in 1808 in celebration of the return from exile of the royal couple Friedrich Wilhelm III and Queen Luise.

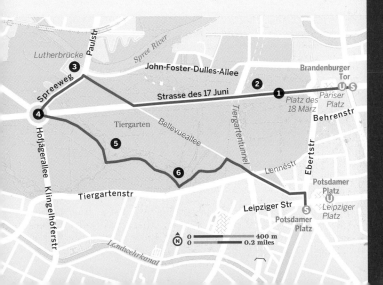

Best
Museums

With more museums than rainy days (around 180 at last count), Berlin has an extraordinarily diverse cultural landscape that caters for just about every interest, be it art, film, history, nature, computers, antiquities or even *Currywurst* (a local snack). Many of them are considered must-see attractions – and not just on rainy days.

BPK · BILDAGENTUR FÜR KUNST, KULTUR UND GESCHICHTE / CLAUDIO DIVIZIA/SHUTTERSTOCK ©

Museum Island

Museum Island (Museumsinsel), a Unesco World Heritage site, presents 6000 years of art and cultural history in five massive repositories. Marvel at antiquities at the Pergamonmuseum and Altes Museum, meet Egyptian queen Nefertiti at the Neues Museum, take in 19th-century art at the Alte Nationalgalerie and admire medieval sculptures at the Bode-Museum.

History Museums

From its humble medieval beginnings, Berlin's history – and especially its key role in major events of the 20th century – is a rich and endlessly fascinating tapestry. It's also extremely well documented, in numerous museums, memorial sites and monuments, many of them in original historic locations and most of them free.

Nationalgalerie Berlin

The National Gallery is a top-ranked collection of mostly European art from the 19th century to today, presented in six locations. The Alte Nationalgalerie specialises in neoclassical, romantic, impressionist and early modernist art; at the Hamburger Bahnhof the spotlight is on international contemporary art; the Museum Berggruen focuses on Picasso; and the Sammlung Scharf-Gerstenberg on surrealist art.

☑ Top Tips

▶ For many museums, you can buy tickets online, allowing you to skip the queues.

▶ Museum lovers should invest in the Museumspass Berlin (€24; available at participating museums and the tourist offices) for one-time entry to about 50 museums on three consecutive days.

Best History Museums

Deutsches Historisches Museum Comprehensive journey through 2000 years of Germany's turbulent past. (p32)

Jüdisches Museum Goes beyond the Holo-

Left: Neues Museum; Above: Ishtar Gate, Pergamonmuseum

caust in tracing the history of Jews in Germany. (p62)

DDR Museum Engaging look at daily life behind the Iron Curtain. (p49)

Best Niche Museums

Bröhan Museum Beautiful objects and furniture from the art deco, art nouveau and functionalist periods. (p100)

Museum für Naturkunde Meet giant dinos in Berlin's own 'Jurassic Park'. (p78)

Museum für Film und Fernsehen An entertaining romp through German celluloid history. (p61)

Museum für Fotografie Spotlight on fashion and lifestyle photographer Helmut Newton. (p91)

Best Antiquities

Pergamonmuseum Treasure trove of monumental architecture from ancient civilisations. (p42)

Altes Museum Gorgeous Schinkel building sheltering priceless antique art and sculpture. (p50)

Neues Museum Pay your respects to Egyptian queen Nefertiti and her entourage. (p46)

Worth a Trip

The **Stasimuseum** (☏ 030-553 6854; www.stasimuseum.de; Haus 1, Ruschestrasse 103; adult/concession €6/4.50; ⊗10am-6pm Mon-Fri, 11am-6pm Sat & Sun; Ⓤ Magdalenenstrasse) provides an overview of the structure, methods and impact of the Ministry of State Security (Stasi), former East Germany's secret police, in its original headquarters. Highlights include surveillance devices, a prisoner transport van and the offices of Stasi chief Erich Mielke.

Best **Architecture**

After visiting the German capital in 1891, Mark Twain remarked, 'Berlin is the newest city I've ever seen'. True then, still true now. Destruction and division have ensured that today's city is essentially a creation of modern times, a showcase of 20th-century styles with few surviving vestiges of earlier times.

Post-Reunification

Reunification presented Berlin with both the challenge and the opportunity to redefine itself architecturally. With the Wall gone, huge gashes of empty space opened where the city's halves were to be rejoined. The grandest of the post-1990 developments is Potsdamer Platz, a contemporary interpretation of the famous historic square. Other recent architectural standouts include the Bundeskanzleramt (Federal Chancellery) and the Jüdisches Museum.

The Schinkel Touch

It was Karl Friedrich Schinkel (1781–1841) who stamped his imprimatur on the face of Prussian Berlin. The most prominent architect of German neoclassicism, he strove for the perfect balance between functionality and beauty, achieved through clear lines, symmetry and an impeccable sense of aesthetics.

The 1920s & the Bauhaus

The spirit of innovation brought some of the finest avant-garde architects to Berlin in the 1920s, including Le Corbusier, Ludwig Mies van der Rohe and Hans Scharoun. Their association later evolved into the Bauhaus, which used practical anti-elitist principles to unite form and function and had a profound effect on modern aesthetics.

Best of Schinkel

Altes Museum The grand colonnaded front inspired by a philosopher's school in Athens is considered Schinkel's most mature work. (p50)

Konzerthaus Berlin A sweeping staircase leads to a raised columned portico in this famous concert hall. (p38)

Neue Wache This royal guardhouse turned antiwar memorial was Schinkel's first Berlin commission. (p35)

Best Prussian

Schloss Charlottenburg Pretty Prussian power display inspired by Versailles and backed by a lavish park. (p99)

Schloss Sanssouci Frederick the Great's rococo retreat where he

Left: Oak Gallery, Schloss Charlottenburg; Above: Berliner Dom

could be 'without cares'. (p141)

Berliner Dom This former royal court church in exuberant Italian Renaissance style overlooks the Spree River. (p49)

Best Post-WWII

Berliner Philharmonie This eccentric concert hall is Hans Scharoun's modernist masterpiece. (p69)

Haus der Kulturen der Welt Avant-garde structure with gravity-defying sculptural roof. (p35)

Neue Nationalgalerie Mies van der Rohe's glass-and-steel cube perches on a granite podium and is lidded by a floating steel-ribbed roof. (p69)

Best Contemporary

Jüdisches Museum Daniel Libeskind's zigzag-shaped architectural metaphor for Jewish history. (p62)

Neues Museum David Chipperfield's reconstructed New Museum ingeniously blends old and new. (p46)

Sony Center Helmut Jahn's svelte glass-and-steel complex is the most striking on Potsdamer Platz. (p61)

Bundeskanzleramt Germany's chancellor steers the country from this riverside 'white house' with lots of sharp angles and circular cutouts. (p25)

Worth a Trip

Built for the 1936 Olympic Games, Berlin's coliseum-style **Olympiastadion** (Olympic Stadium; ☎030-2500 2322; www.olympiastadion-berlin.de; Olympischer Platz 3; adult/concession self-guided tour €7/5.50, highlights tour €11/9.50; ⏱9am-7pm Apr-Jul, Sep & Oct, 9am-8pm Aug, 10am-4pm Nov-Mar; ⑤Olympiastadion, Ⓤ Olympiastadion) was revamped for the 2006 FIFA World Cup and now sports a spidery oval roof, snazzy VIP boxes and top sound, lighting and projection systems.

Best
Historical Sites

In Berlin the past is always present. Strolling around boulevards and neighbourhoods, you can't help but pass legendary sights that take you back to the era of Prussian glory, the dark ages of the Third Reich, the tense period of the Cold War and the euphoria of reunification.

USCHOOLS UNIVERSITY IMAGES/GETTY IMAGES ©

The Age of Prussia

Berlin has been a royal residence ever since Elector Friedrich III was elevated to King Friedrich I in 1701. This promotion significantly shaped the city, which blossomed under Frederick the Great, who sought greatness as much on the battlefield as through building. In the 19th century, Prussia weathered revolutions and industrialisation to forge the creation of the German Reich, which lasted until the monarchy's demise in 1918.

The Third Reich

No other political power shaped the 20th century as much as Nazi Germany. The megalomania of Hitler and his henchmen wrought destruction upon much of Europe, bringing death to at least 50 million people, and forever realigned the world order. Few original sites remain, but memorials and museums keep the horror in focus.

Cold War Chills

After WWII, Germany fell into the crosshairs of the Cold War, a country divided along ideological lines by the victorious powers, its internal border marked by fences and a wall. Just how differently the two countries developed is still palpable in Berlin, expressed not only through Berlin Wall remnants such as the East Side Gallery but also through vastly different urban planning and architectural styles.

Best of Prussian Pomp

Brandenburg Gate This much photographed triumphal arch is Germany's most iconic national symbol. (p26)

Reichstag Stand in awe of history at the palatial home of the German parliament. (p24)

Schloss Charlottenburg Sumptuous palace provides a glimpse into the lifestyles of the rich and royal. (p99)

Schloss & Park Sanssouci King Frederick the Great built this charming royal retreat in the nearby town of Potsdam. (p141)

Berliner Dom The royal court church has impressive dimensions, stunning acoustics and elaborately carved sarcophagi for the remains

Left: The Reichstag dome; Above: East Side Gallery

of kings and queens. (p49)

Best of Red Berlin

Gedenkstätte Berliner Mauer Indoor-outdoor multimedia exhibit which vividly illustrates the history, physical appearance and impact of the Berlin Wall. (p131)

Tränenpalast Explains why tears of goodbye once flowed in this Friedrichstrasse border pavilion. (p32)

East Side Gallery The longest remaining stretch of Berlin Wall turned art canvas by more than 100 artists. (p120)

Karl-Marx-Allee East Berlin's pompous yet impressive main boulevard

and showpiece of socialist architecture. (p124)

Best of WWII History

Topographie des Terrors Gripping examination of the origins of Nazism, its perpetrators and its victims, on the site of the SS and Gestapo headquarters. (p65)

Holocaust Memorial Commemorates the unspeakable horrors of the WWII Jewish genocide. (p28)

Gedenkstätte Deutscher Widerstand Commemorates the brave men and women of the German Nazi resistance. (p65)

Worth a Trip

Victims of persecution by the GDR-era Ministry of State Security (Stasi) often ended up at the grim **Stasi Prison** (Gedenkstätte Berlin-Hohenschönhausen; www.stiftung-hsh.de; Genslerstrasse 66; tours adult/concession €6/3, exhibit free; ⏰tours in English 10.30am, 12.30pm & 2.30pm Mar-Oct, 2.30pm daily & 11.30am Sat & Sun Nov-Feb, exhibit 9am-6pm, German tours more frequent; 🚋M5). Tours reveal the full extent of the terror and cruelty perpetrated upon thousands of suspected regime opponents, many utterly innocent.

Best
Tours

If you're a Berlin first-timer, letting someone else show you around is a great way to get your bearings, see the key sights quickly and obtain a general understanding of the city. All manner of explorations – from generic city bus tours to special-interest outings – are available.

Walking & Cycling Tours

Several companies offer English-language general city explorations and themed tours (eg Third Reich, Cold War, Potsdam) that don't require reservations – you just show up at the designated meeting point. Since these may change, check online for the latest or look for flyers in hotel or hostel lobbies. Some guides work for tips only but the better tours cost between €12 and €20.

Boat Tours

On a warm day, it's fun to see Berlin from the deck of a boat cruising the city's rivers, canals and lakes. Tours range from one-hour spins around the historic centre to longer trips to Schloss Charlottenburg and beyond. Most operators offer live commentary in English and German and sell refreshments on board. Embarkation points cluster around Museum Island or check the website of **Stern und Kreisschiffahrt** (☏030-536 3600; www.sternundkreis.de; ◷Mar-Dec) for other locations.

Bus Tours

Colourful buses tick off the key sights on two-hour loops with basic taped commentary in multiple languages. You're free to get off and back on at any of the stops. They depart roughly every 15 or 30 minutes between 10am and 5pm or 6pm daily; tickets cost €10 to €20. Several companies have a terminus along Kurfürstendamm.

JEAN-PIERRE LESCOURRET/GETTY IMAGES ©

☑ Top Tips

▶ Get a crash course in 'Berlin-ology' by hopping on public bus 100 or 200 at Zoologischer Garten or Alexanderplatz and letting the sights whoosh by for the price of an AB transport ticket.

▶ For a DIY tour of the Berlin Wall follow the Berliner Mauerweg (Berlin Wall Trail) with 40 multilingual information stations posted along the way.

Best Cycling & Walking Tours

Alternative Berlin Tours (☏0162 819 8264; www.alternativeberlin.com; tours €10-20) Roster includes tip-based subculture tours, a street-art tour

Boat cruise on the Spree River

and workshop, an alternative pub crawl and a craft-beer tour.

Fat Tire Tours Berlin

(📞 030-2404 7991; www. fattiretours.com/berlin; Panoramastrasse 1a; adult/ concession/under 12 incl bicycle from €28/26/14; **S** Alexanderplatz, **U** Alexanderplatz) Various themed English-language tours focus on Nazi Germany, the Cold War or 'Modern Berlin'.

Original Berlin Walks

(📞 030-301 9194; www. berlinwalks.de; adult/ concession from €14/12) Berlin's longest-running English-language walking tour company has a large roster of general and themed tours.

Brewer's Berlin Tours

(📞 0177 388 1537; www. brewersberlintours.com;

adult/concession €15/12) Epic six-hour city tour plus themed tours on craft beer, spies and Potsdam.

Best Speciality Tours

Berlin Music Tours

(📞 030-3087 5633; www. musictours-berlin.com; Bowie walk €14; ⏰ Bowie walk noon-3pm Sun) Bowie to U2, Rammstein to the Love Parade, this outfit brings alive Berlin's storied music history.

Berliner Unterwelten

(📞 030-4991 0517; www. berliner-unterwelten.de; Brunnenstrasse 105; adult/ concession €11/9; ⏰ Dark Worlds tours in English 1pm Mon & 11am Thu-Mon year-round, 11am Wed Mar-Nov, 3pm Wed-Mon & 1pm Wed-

Sun Apr-Oct; **S** Gesundbrunnen, **U** Gesundbrunnen) Pick your way past heavy steel doors, hospital beds, helmets, guns and other WWII artefacts on a tour of WWII-era bunkers, shelters and tunnels.

Berlinagenten

(📞 030-4372 0701; www.berlin agenten.com; tours from €200) Get a handle on all facets of Berlin's urban lifestyle with an insider private guide who opens doors to hot and/or secret locations.

Eat the World

(📞 030-206 229 990; www.eat-the-world.com; tours €33) Berlin one bite at a time on three-hour culinary sightseeing tours with stops at cafes, delis, bakeries and more.

Best
Art

Art aficionados will find their compass on perpetual spin in Berlin. Home to 440 galleries, scores of world-class collections and some 33,000 international artists, it has assumed a pole position on the global artistic circuit. Adolescent energy, restlessness and experimental spirit combined and infused with an undercurrent of grit are what give this 'eternally unfinished' city its street cred.

Commercial Art Galleries

The Galleries Association of Berlin (www.berliner-galerien.de) counts some 400 galleries within the city. In addition, there are at least 200 noncommercial showrooms and off-spaces that regularly show new exhibitions. Although the orientation is global, it's well worth keeping an eye out for the latest works by major contemporary artists living and working in Berlin, including Thomas Demand, Jonathan Meese, Via Lewandowsky, Isa Genzken, Tino Sehgal, Esra Ersen, John Bock and the artist duo Ingar Dragset and Michael Elmgreen.

Galleries cluster in four main areas: around Auguststrasse and Linienstrasse in the Scheunenviertel; around Checkpoint Charlie (eg Zimmerstrasse, Markgrafenstrasse); on Potsdamer Strasse in Schöneberg; and around Savignyplatz near Kurfürstendamm.

Public Art

Free installations, sculptures and paintings? Absolutely. Public art is big in Berlin, which happens to be home to the world's longest outdoor mural, the 1.3km-long East Side Gallery (p120). No matter which neighbourhood you walk in, you're going to encounter public art on a grand scale.

MAGMAC83/SHUTTERSTOCK ©

☑ Top Tips

▶ Blockbuster visiting shows often sell out so it's best to prepurchase tickets online. Same goes for Pergamonmuseum and Neues Museum.

▶ Most private collections require advance registration; reserve months ahead for the Sammlung Boros.

▶ The Museumspass Berlin (€24) buys entry to about 50 museums for three consecutive days. Sold at tourist offices and participating museums.

Left: DaimlerCity Complex, Potsdamer Platz area; Above: Sammlung Boros

Best Art Museums

Gemäldegalerie Sweeping survey of Old Masters from Germany, Italy, France, Spain and the Netherlands from the 13th to the 18th centuries. (p56)

Sammlung Boros Book months ahead for tickets to see this stunning cutting-edge private collection housed in a WWII bunker. (p78)

Alte Nationalgalerie Showcase of first-rate 19th-century art by leading German romantics and realists. (p50)

Best Niche Collections

Museum Berggruen Priceless Picassos, plus works by Klee and Giacometti. (p100)

Sammlung Scharf-Gerstenberg Enter the surreal worlds conjured up by Goya, Max Ernst, Magritte and other giants of the genre. (p100)

Best Contemporary Art

Hamburger Bahnhof Warhol, Beuys and Twombly are among the many legends aboard the contemporary-art express at this former train station. (p78)

Sammlung Boros The latest works by established and emerging artists displayed in a labyrinthine WWII bunker. (p78)

Deutsche Bank Kunst-Halle Shines the spotlight on the art scene in emerging countries and examines the effects of globalisation on the art world. (p33)

Best for Public Art

Daimler Contemporary Berlin In the Potsdamer Platz area, DaimlerCity offers especially rich pickings with works by Keith Haring, Mark Di Suvero and Frank Stella. (p61)

Best
Eating

If you crave traditional German comfort food, you'll certainly find plenty of places to indulge in pork knuckles, smoked pork chops and calf's liver in Berlin. These days, though, 'typical' local fare is lighter, healthier, more creative, and more likely to come from an organic eatery, an ethnic restaurant or a gourmet kitchen (including 20 flaunting 26 Michelin stars between them).

GKRPHOTO/SHUTTERSTOCK ©

Modern Regional Cuisine

The organic, slow-food and locavore movements are stronger than ever in Berlin with such ingredients as apple-fed pork from the Havelland, fish from the Müritz Lake District or wild boar from the Schorfheide showing up on menus around Berlin.

Street Food

Street food and food trucks have been part of Berlin's culinary scene for years now, not just in random locations at markets and events around town but also at regular gatherings. Still going strong is **Street Food Thursday** (p112) at Markthalle Neun, the year-round event that started the craze back in 2013. From spring to autumn, it is joined by a number of alfresco schemes like **Bite Club** (www.biteclub.de; Arena Berlin, Eichenstrasse 4; 🕔5pm–midnight every 3rd Fri May-Sep; 🚇Treptower Park, 🚇Schlesisches Tor) and **Burgers & Hip Hop** (www.facebook.com/burgersandhiphop; Prinzenstrasse 85f; 🕔3pm–6am Sat, dates vary; 🚇Moritzplatz).

Local Fast Food

A cult snack is the *Currywurst,* a fried or grilled *Wiener* sliced into bite-sized ringlets, swimming in a spicy tomato sauce and dusted with curry powder. The doner kebab was allegedly invented by a Turkish immigrant in 1970s West Berlin.

☑ Top Tips

▶ Reservations are essential at the top eateries and are recommended for midrange restaurants – especially for dinner and at weekends.

▶ It's customary to add between 5% and 10% for good service.

Best Traditional German

Augustiner am Gendarmenmarkt Go the whole hog at this famous Munich beer-hall transplant. (p35)

Schwarzwaldstuben Oldies but goodies from Germany's south amid delightfully irreverent decor. (p82)

Left: *Currywurst;* Above: Max und Moritz

Max und Moritz
Industrial-weight platters and local brews in charmingly decorated centenarian pub. (p110)

Best Asian

Chutnify South Indian street food so perky it may get you off your Prozac. (p134)

Umami Modern Vietnamese food that sings with freshness and creativity. (p136)

Good Friends Top Chinese restaurant delivers a taste-bud tingling culinary journey. (p93)

Best Quick Feeds

Burgermeister This patty-and-bun joint in a historic toilet is a hugely popular pit stop on a budget. (p110)

Habba Habba Hole-in-the-wall stuffs Middle Eastern wraps with unexpected meatless ingredients. (p135)

Konnopke's Imbiss Sausage kitchen with cult status. (p136)

Best Vegetarian

Lucky Leek Richly satisfying meatfree dishes in stylish-minimalist setting. (p137)

Cookies Cream Clandestine meatfree kitchen tiptoes between hip and haute. (p36)

Hummus & Friends Hip Tel Aviv import makes kosher hummus and more next to the New Synagogue. (p81)

Best Michelin Eats

Restaurant Tim Raue The outpost by Berlin's rebel turned top toque ranks among the best 50 in the world. (p66)

Restaurant Richard Arty decor combines with supreme classic French cooking in this relaxed gourmet lair. (p111)

Pauly Saal Time-honoured regional dishes reinterpreted in modern Michelin-decorated fashion. (p82)

Best
Shopping

EQROY/SHUTTERSTOCK ©

Berlin is a great place to shop, and we're definitely not talking malls and chains. The city's appetite for the individual manifests in small neighbourhood boutiques and buzzing markets that are a pleasure to explore. Shopping here is as much about visual stimulus as it is about actually spending your cash, no matter whether you're ultrafrugal or a power-shopper.

Where to Shop

Berlin's main shopping boulevard is Kurfürstendamm (Ku'damm) in the City West, which is largely the purview of mainstream retailers (from H&M to Prada). Its extension, Tauentzienstrasse, is anchored by KaDeWe, continental Europe's largest department store. Standouts among the city's shopping centres are the concept mall Bikini Berlin and the vast LP12 Mall of Berlin at Leipziger Platz.

Getting the most out of shopping in Berlin, though, means venturing off the high street and into the *Kieze* (neighbourhoods), which are filled with a cosmopolitan cocktail of indie boutiques.

Opening Hours

Malls, department stores and supermarkets are open 9.30am to 8pm or 9pm; some supermarkets are 24 hours. Boutiques and other smaller shops have flexible hours, usually from 11am to 7pm weekdays, and to 4pm or 5pm Saturday. One handy feature of Berlin culture is the *Spätkauf* (*Späti* in local vernacular), which are small neighbourhood stores stocked with the basics and open from early evening until 2am or later.

☑ Top Tips

▶ Most stores, especially smaller ones, don't accept credit cards.

▶ On Sundays, head to Berlin's fabulous flea markets.

Best Markets

Flohmarkt am Mauerpark The mother of all markets is overrun but still a good show. (p131)

Türkischer Markt Bazaar-like canal-side market with bargain-priced produce and Mediterranean deli fare. (p117)

Flohmarkt am Boxhagener Platz Fun finds are bound to abound at this charmer on a leafy square. (p127)

Left: Galeries Lafayette; Above: Bikini Berlin

Best Gastro Delights

KaDeWe Food Hall
Mind-boggling bonanza of gourmet treats from around the world. (p96)

Street Food Thursday
Global bites in a revitalised 19th-century market hall bring in foodies every Thursday evening. (p112)

Rausch Schokoladenhaus Palace of pralines and chocolate, plus ingenious model-sized chocolate replicas of famous Berlin landmarks. (p38)

Best Malls & Department Stores

Bikini Berlin The city's first concept mall with hip stores and views of the monkeys at Berlin Zoo. (p97)

LP12 Mall of Berlin
Huge high-end shopping quarter with 270 stores alongside apartments, a hotel and offices. (p69)

Galeries Lafayette
French *je ne sais quois* in überstylish building by Jean Nouvel. (p39)

Best Gifts & Souvenirs

Ampelmann Berlin
Berlin's cute 'traffic-light man' graces everything from bibs to bags. Multiple branches. (p85)

Bonbonmacherei Willy Wonka would feel right at home in this old-fashioned candy kitchen. (p84)

Käthe Wohlfahrt
It's Christmas time 365/24/7 at this emporium of baubles, decorations and ornaments. (p97)

Best Quirky Stores

1. Absinth Depot Berlin
Make your acquaintance with the Green Fairy at this quaint Old Berlin–style shop. (p85)

VEB Orange Ramshackle treasure trove packed with finds from communist times. (p139)

Frau Tonis Parfum
Smell like Marlene or Angela with heady potions blended in Berlin at this bijou boutique. (p39)

Best
Bars

As one of Europe's primo party capitals, Berlin offers a thousand and one scenarios for getting your cocktails and kicks (or wine or beer, for that matter). From cocktail lairs and rooftop lounges to concept and craft-beer pubs – the next thirst parlor is usually within stumbling distance.

MARK READ/LONELY PLANET ©

Etiquette

Table service is common, and you shouldn't order at the bar unless you intend to hang out there or there's a sign saying *Selbstbedienung* (self-service). In traditional German pubs, it's customary to keep a tab instead of paying for each round separately. In bars with DJs a 'tip' of €2 is usually added to the cost of your first drink. Tip bartenders about 5%, servers 10%. Drinking in public is legal and widely practised, especially around party zones. Try to be civilised about it, though. No puking on the U-Bahn, please!

What's Pouring?

Not surprisingly, beer – especially Pils and Weizenbier (wheat beer) – is big in Berlin and most places pour a variety of national and imported brews. In general, though, locally produced craft beers are gaining in popularity with pioneers including Heidenpeters, Vagabund and Hops & Barley, all with their own tap rooms. Also look for vodka by Our/Berlin; Korn (a premium schnapps) by Berliner Brandstifter; or cider by Original Berliner Cidre. A new crop of dedicated wine bars and cocktail caverns has also notably elevated the 'liquid art' scene of late.

☑ **Top Tips**

▶ The line between cafe and bar is often blurred, with many changing stripes as the hands move around the clock.

▶ Alcohol is served (and consumed) pretty much all day. Some bars have happy hours that usually run from 6pm to 9pm.

Best Craft-Beer Pubs

Hops & Barley Fabulous unfiltered pilsner, dark and wheat beer made in a former butcher's shop. (p126)

Hopfenreich Berlin's first craft-beer bar also has tastings, tap take-

Strandbar Mitte

overs and guest brewers. (p113)

Pier This upscale craft-beer bar inspired by Coney Island also serves American snacks. (p83)

Best Cocktail Bars

Schwarze Traube Pint-sized drinking parlour with bespoke cocktails. (p112)

Würgeengel Fun crowd keeps the cocktails and conversation flowing in a genuine '50s setting. (p107)

Thelonius Perfect trifecta of soft sounds, lovely light and expert cocktails. (p117)

Becketts Kopf Wait for Godot while sipping supreme classics and

seasonal inspirations. (p138)

Buck and Breck Cocktail classics for grown-ups in a speakeasy-style setting. (p83)

Best Beer Gardens

Prater Biergarten Berlin's oldest beer garden still rocks beneath the chestnuts after 175 years in business. (p137)

Cafe am Neuen See Beer and pretzels by a pond in a romantic setting in Tiergarten park. (p150)

Best Wine Bars

Otto Rink For relaxed but demanding wine fans

with a penchant for German wines. (p107)

Weinerei Forum Works on the honour system: you drink, then decide how much to pay. (p137)

Best Summertime Bars

Klunkerkranich Hipster spot with urban garden and great sunset views atop Neukölln shopping centre. (p117)

Strandbar Mitte Berlin's original beach bar with views of Museum Island. (p52)

Club der Visionäre Boatshed turned party pen with DJs who know the groove. (p112)

Best Clubs

Berlin is Germany's club capital, the city where techno came of age, the living heart of the European electronic scene and the spiritual home of the lost weekend. With a sound spectrum from minimal techno to fist-pumping hip-hop and tango, finding a party to match your mood shouldn't be a tall order.

The Berlin Scene

What distinguishes the Berlin scene from other party capitals is a focus on independent, non-mainstream niche venues, run by owners or collectives with a creative background. The shared goal is to promote a diverse, inclusive and progressive club culture rather than to maximise profit.

When to Go

Berlin's famously long nights have gotten even later and, thanks to a growing number of after parties and daytime clubs, not going home at all is definitely an option at weekends. Savvy clubbers put in a good night's sleep, then hit the dance floor when other people head for Sunday church or afternoon tea.

At the Door

Doors are notoriously tough at Berlin's best clubs (eg Watergate, Berghain/Panorama Bar, Salon zur Wilden Renate) as door staff strive to sift out people that would feel uncomfortable with the music, the vibe or the libertine ways past the door. Except at some disco-type establishments, flaunting fancy labels and glam cocktail dresses can actually get in the way of your getting in. Wear something black and casual. If your attitude is right, age rarely matters. As elsewhere, large groups have a lower chance of getting in, so split up if you can. Stag and hen parties are rarely welcome at the better clubs.

☑ Top Tips

▶ The wildest parties are staged off-grid in such outer boroughs as Lichtenberg, Treptow and Wedding.

▶ If you have to queue, be respectful, don't drink and don't talk too loudly (seriously!). Don't arrive wasted.

▶ Don't bother showing up before 1am unless you want to have a deep conversation with a bored bartender.

Left: Nightclub in RAW Gelände (p126); Above: Clärchens Ballhaus

Best for Electro

Berghain/Panorama Bar Big bad Berghain is still the best in town. (p125)

://about blank Gritty techno hot spot with enchanting summer garden. (p126)

Salon zur wilden Renate Psychedelic home of flashy-trashy electro parties in an abandoned apartment building. (p126)

Ritter Butzke Low-key but high-calibre electro club in ex-factory keeps it real with mostly local DJs and a crowd that appreciates them. (p112)

Best Non-Electro

Clärchens Ballhaus Hipsters mix it up with grannies for tango and jitterbug in a kitsch-glam 1913 ballroom. (p83)

Kaffee Burger Home of the 'Russian Disco', readings and garage band concerts. (p83)

Best Outdoor Partying

Club der Visionäre Summers wouldn't be the same without chilling and dancing in this historic canal-side boatshed. (p112)

Worth a Trip

On summer weekends, **Sisyphos** (📞030-9836 6839; www.sisyphos-berlin. net; Hauptstrasse 15; ⏱hours vary, usually midnight Fri-10am Mon Jun-Aug, weather permitting; 🚋21, Ⓢ Ostkreuz) in a former dog-food factory about 2km southeast of Ostkreuz S-Bahn station turns into an open-air nonstop party village from Friday midnight through Monday morning. Techno and tech house dominate the turntables. Tram 21 to Gustav-Holzmann-Strasse will get you close.

Best
LGBT

Berlin's legendary liberalism has spawned one of the world's biggest, most divine and diverse LGBT playgrounds. Anything goes in 'Homopolis' (and we do mean anything!), from the highbrow to the hands-on, the bourgeois to the bizarre, the mainstream to the flamboyant. Except for the most hard-core places, gay spots get their share of opposite-sex and straight patrons.

LGBT Community

The area around Nollendorfplatz in Schöneberg (Motzstrasse and Fuggerstrasse especially) has been a gay mecca since the 1920s. Institutions like Tom's, Hafen and Connection pull in the punters nightly, and there's also plenty of nocturnal action for the leather and fetish set. Current hipster central is Kreuzberg, which teems with party pens, especially along Oranienstrasse and Mehringdamm, though none are exclusively gay. Across the river, Friedrichshain has a couple of gay bars alongside gay fave Berghain/Panorama Bar and the hardcore Lab.oratory. Old East Berlin's pink hub Prenzlauer Berg has a few low-key cafes and hardcore cruising dens.

LGBT Partying

Generally speaking, Berlin's gayscape runs the entire spectrum from mellow cafes, campy bars and cinemas to saunas, cruising areas, clubs with darkrooms and all-out sex venues. In fact, sex and sexuality are entirely everyday matters to the unshockable city folks and there are very few, if any, itches that can't be quite openly and legally scratched. As elsewhere, gay men have more options for having fun, but grrrrls of all stripes won't feel left out either.

ALEXANDER H. SCHULZ/GETTY IMAGES ©

☑ **Top Tips**

▸ Siegessäule (www. siegessaeule.de) is the free weekly lesbigay 'bible'.

▸ Out in Berlin (www. out-in-berlin.com) is a free up-to-date English/German booklet and website, often found at tourist offices.

▸ The Queer Berlin tour (www. berlinwalks.de) through Kreuzberg and Schöneberg taps into the city's LGBT legacy.

Parade during Christopher Street Day, Berlin's gay pride celebration

Best Clubs & Parties

GMF Glamtastic Sunday club with pretty people in stylish and central location. (p53)

Chantals House of Shame Eponymous trash-drag diva's weekly parties at Bassy run wild and wicked. (p138)

SchwuZ LGBT club with different theme parties – great for scene newbies.

Best Bars & Pubs

Roses Plush, pink, campy madhouse – an essential late-night stop on a lesbigay bar hop. (p107)

Möbel Olfe Old furniture shop recast as busy drinking den; Thursdays are especially busy. (p106)

Himmelreich This '50s retro lounge is a lesbigay-scene stalwart in Friedrichshain. (p127)

Best Sex Clubs

Greifbar Friendly cruising bar in Prenzlauer Berg with video, darkroom and private areas. (p139)

Worth a Trip

In a former brewery in Neukölln, queer party institution **SchwuZ** (☎ 030-5770 2270; www.schwuz.de; Rollbergstrasse 26; ⊙ from 11pm Thu-Sat; ☒ 104, 167, Ⓤ Rathaus Neukölln) is the go-to spot for high-energy flirting and dancing. Different nightly parties draw different punters, so check what's on before heading out. Regular parties include Electronic Thursdays and the L-Tunes lesbian party. Good for easing into Berlin's LGBT party scene.

Best
Music &
Performance

CHRISTIAN MARQUARDT/CONTRIBUTOR/GETTY IMAGES ©

Berlin's performing arts scene is lively, edgy and the richest and most varied in the German-speaking world. With three state-supported opera houses, five major orchestras – including the world-class Berliner Philharmoniker – scores of theatres, cinemas, cabarets and concert venues, you've got enough entertainment options to last you a lifetime.

Best Classical Music

Berliner Philharmonie One of the world's top orchestras within its own 'cathedral of sound'. (p69)

Staatsoper im Schiller Theater Top-ranked opera house. (p96)

Best Cabaret

Chamäleon Varieté Historic variety theatre in the Hackesche Höfe presents mesmerising contemporary spins on acrobatics, dance, theatre, magic and music. (p84)

Bar Jeder Vernunft An art nouveau mirrored tent provides a suitably glam backdrop for high-quality entertainment. (p96)

Friedrichstadt-Palast Europe's largest revue theatre is the realm of leggy dancers and Vegas-worthy technology. (p84)

Tipi am Kanzleramt There's not a bad seat in the house at this festive dinner theatre in a tent on the edge of the Tiergarten park. (p38)

Best Live Music

Lido Head-bobbing platform for indie bands, big names included. (p115)

Astra Kulturhaus Clued-in bookers fill this rambling space with everything from big-name artists to electro swing parties. (p127)

Wild at Heart Friendly biker-style dive with loud music and cheap beers. (p115)

☑ Top Tips

▶ Early bookings are always advisable but essential in the case of the Berliner Philharmoniker, the Staatsoper and big-name concerts.

▶ Many theatres are closed on Mondays and in July and August

▶ Indie concerts and events can be booked at **Koka 36** (☎030-6110 1313; www.koka36.de; Oranienstrasse 29; ⏱9am-7pm Mon-Fri, 10am-4pm Sat; ⓊKottbusser Tor).

A-Trane Occasionally hosts jazz A-listers and has a rollicking Saturday-night jam session. (p96)

Best
Quiet Spots

If your head is spinning with all the stimulus Berlin is throwing at you, there are plenty of places that can provide a restorative antidote. Fantastic outdoor spots and serene retreats await in every neighbourhood.

JEAN-PIERRE LESCOURRET/GETTY IMAGES ©

Best Parks & Gardens

Schlossgarten Charlottenburg Set up a picnic near the carp pond and ponder royal splendours. (p98)

Park Sanssouci Find your favourite spot away from the crowds in this sprawling royal park. (p140)

Volkspark Friedrichshain Sprawling 'people's park' with hills created from WWII rubble. (p124)

Best Memorial Sites

Neue Wache An antiwar memorial centred on an emotional Käthe Kollwitz sculpture. (p35)

Holocaust Memorial An outsized maze of stelae represents this outsized crime against humanity. (p28)

Luftbrückendenkmal Pay tribute to a true 'triumph of the will' at the Berlin Airlift Memorial. (p71)

Best Churches

Berliner Dom Royal court church cutting a commanding presence on Museum Island. (p49)

Kaiser-Wilhelm-Gedächtniskirche Bombed-out church serves as poignant reminder of the futility of war. (p90)

☑ **Top Tips**

▸ Get lost amid the restful expanse of lawns, trees and paths of the enormous **Tiergarten** (p150), one of the world's largest urban parks and popular for strolling, jogging, picnicking, Frisbee tossing and, yes, nude sunbathing. It's sprinkled with monuments, beer gardens, ponds and historical markers.

Best
With Kids

ANTICIOLO/SHUTTERSTOCK ©

Travelling to Berlin with kids can be child's play, especially if you keep a light schedule and involve them in day-to-day planning. There's plenty to do to keep youngsters occupied, from zoos to kid-oriented museums. Parks and imaginative playgrounds abound in all neighbourhoods, as do public pools.

Museum für Naturkunde Meet giant dinosaurs, travel through space back to the beginning of time and find out why zebras are striped in this wonderful museum. (p78)

Legoland Discovery Centre Geared towards the primary-school set, this cute indoor amusement park counts a 4D cinema, a Lego space station and a slow-mo ride through the Dragon Castle among its attractions. (☑01806-6669 0110; www.legolanddiscoverycentre.de/berlin; Potsdamer Strasse 4; €18.50; ☺10am-7pm, last admission 5pm; ☐200, Ⓢ Potsdamer Platz, ⓊPotsdamer Platz)

Science Center Spectrum Play with, experience and learn about such concepts as bal-ance, weight, water, air and electricity in dozens of hands-on science experiments. (☑030-9025 4284; www.sdtb.de; Möckernstrasse 26; adult/concession/under 18 €8/4/free after 3pm; ☺9am-5.30pm Tue-Fri, 10am-6pm Sat & Sun; ⓊMöckernbrücke, Gleisdreieck)

Deutsches Technikmuseum This giant shrine to technology counts the world's first computer, an entire hall of vintage locomotives and extensive exhibits on aerospace and navigation among its top attractions. (German Museum of Technology; ☑030-902 540; www.sdtb.de; Trebbiner Strasse 9; adult/concession/under 18 €8/4/after 3pm free, audioguide adult/concession €2/1; ☺9am-5.30pm Tue-Fri, 10am-6pm Sat & Sun; ⓊGleisdreieck, Möckernbrücke)

Computerspielemuseum A fascinating trip down computer-game memory lane that also puts the industry's evolution into historical and cultural context. (Computer Games Museum; ☑030-6098 8577; www.computerspielemuseum.de; Karl-Marx-Allee 93a; adult/concession €8/5; ☺10am-8pm; ☐240, 347, ⓊWeberwiese)

Madame Tussauds Kids of any age are all smiles when posing with the waxen likeness of their favourite pop star or celluloid celebrity. (p35)

Berlin Zoo If the 20,000 furry, feathered and finned friends fail to enchant the little ones, there's also always the enormous adventure playground. (p90)

Survival Guide

Survival Guide

Before You Go

When to Go

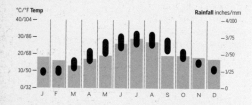

°C/°F Temp
Rainfall inches/mm

➡ Winter (Nov–Feb)
Cold and dark, snow possible. Sights are crowd-free; theatre and concert season in full swing.

➡ Spring (Mar–May)
Mild, often sunny. Sights start getting busier; festival season kicks off; beer gardens and outdoor cafes open.

➡ Summer (Jun–Aug)
Warm to hot, often sunny, thunderstorms possible. Peak tourist season; sights and museums are super-busy; life moves outdoors.

➡ Autumn (Sep–Oct)
Mild, often sunny. Theatre, concert and football (soccer) seasons start up.

Book Your Stay

➡ Berlin has over 137,000 hotel rooms but the most desirable properties book up quickly, especially in summer and around major holidays, festivals and trade shows; prices soar and reservations are essential during these periods.

➡ Otherwise, rates are mercifully low by Western capital standards. Options range from luxurious ports of call to ho-hum international chains, trendy designer boutique hotels to Old Berlin-style B&Bs, happening hostels to handy self-catering apartments.

➡ The most central district is Mitte. Hotels around Kurfürstendamm are plentiful but put you a U-Bahn ride away from most blockbuster sights and nightlife.

➡ Kreuzberg and Friedrichshain are ideal for party animals.

➡ Berlin's hostel scene is as vibrant as ever with dorm beds available from as little as €9.

➡ Value-added tax (VAT; 7%) has long been included in room rates, but since 1 January 2014 an additional 5% 'city tax' is payable on the net room rates, eg excluding VAT and fees for amenities and services. The tax is added to the hotel bill. Business travellers are exempted.

Useful Websites

Lonely Planet (www. lonelyplanet.com/germany/hotels) Lonely Planet's online booking service with insider lowdown on the best places to stay.

Visit Berlin (www.visit berlin.de) Official Berlin tourist office books rooms at partner hotels with a best-price guarantee.

Boutique Hotels Berlin (www.boutiquehotels-berlin. com) Booking service for about 20 hand-picked boutique hotels.

Berlin30 (www.berlin30. com) Online low-cost booking agency for hotels, hostels, apartments and B&Bs.

Best Budget

Grand Hostel Berlin (www.grandhostel-berlin.de) Connect to the magic of yesteryear at this historic lair imbued with both character and modern amenities.

Wombats City Hostel Berlin (www.wombats-hostels.com/berlin) Fun seekers should thrive at this well-run hostel with hip in-house bar.

EastSeven Berlin Hostel (www.eastseven.de) Friendly and low-key hostel with communal vibe ideal for solo travellers.

Plus Berlin (www. plushostels.com/plusberlin) Next-gen hostel with pool in stumbling distance of bar and club central in Friedrichshain.

Best Midrange

Michelberger Hotel (www. michelbergerhotel.com) Fun base with eccentric design, party pedigree and unpretentious vibe.

Brilliant Apartments (www.brilliant-apartments. de) Stylish mash-up of modern and historic in spacious units on trendy street.

Miniloft Berlin (www. miniloft.com) Architect-designed lofts with designer furniture, cozy alcoves and kitchenettes.

Circus Hotel (www.circus-berlin.de) Perennial pleaser thanks to being a perfect synthesis of style, comfort, location and value.

25hours Hotel Bikini Berlin (www.25hours-hotels. com) Inner-city playground with easy access to top shopping and rooms overlooking the Berlin Zoo.

Adina Apartment Hotel Berlin Checkpoint Charlie (www.tfehotels.com/de/brands/adina-apartment-hotels) Ideal base for budget-conscious space-craving self-caterers.

Best Top End

Mandala Hotel (www.the mandala.de) All-suite city slicker with uncluttered urban feel and top eats.

Louisa's Place (www. louisas-place.de) Personal attention is key at this refined outpost with XL-sized suites.

Casa Camper (www. casacamper.com) Infectious irreverence paired with all the zeitgeist essentials global nomads crave.

Das Stue (www.das-stue. com) Charismatic refuge from the urban bustle with understated grandeur and Tiergarten park as a front yard.

Hotel am Steinplatz (www.hotelsteinplatz.com) Golden 1920s glamour radiates from the listed walls of this revivified art-deco jewel.

Arriving in Berlin

From Berlin-Tegel Airport

➜ **Tegel Airport** (TXL; ☎030-6091 1150; www. berlin-airport.de; 🚏 Tegel Flughafen) is about 8km northwest of Zoologischer Garten and 13km northwest of Alexanderplatz.

➜ The TXL express bus connects Tegel to Alexanderplatz (40 minutes) via Hauptbahnhof (central train station) and

Unter den Linden every 10 minutes.

➜ For the City West around Zoologischer Garten take bus X9 (20 minutes), which also runs at 10-minute intervals.

➜ The closest S-Bahn station is Jungfernheide, which is a stop on the S41/S42 (the Ringbahn, or circle line). It is linked to the airport by bus X9.

➜ The closest U-Bahn station is Jakob-Kaiser-Platz, served by bus 109 and X9. From here, the U7 takes you directly to Schöneberg and Kreuzberg.

➜ All journeys cost €2.70 (Tariff AB).

➜ Taxi rides cost about €20 to Zoologischer Garten and €27 to Alexanderplatz and take 30 to 45 minutes. There's a €0.50 airport surcharge.

From Berlin-Schönefeld Airport

➜ **Schönefeld Airport** (SXF; ☎030-6091 1150; www. berlin-airport.de; 🚏 Airport-Express, RE7 & RB14) is about 22km southeast of Alexanderplatz.

➜ The airport train station is 400m from the termi-

nals. Free shuttle buses run every 10 minutes.

➜ Airport-Express trains make the trip to central Berlin twice hourly in 20 to 30 minutes. Note: these are regular regional trains denoted as RE7 and RB14 in timetables.

➜ The slower S-Bahn S9 runs every 20 minutes and is useful if you're headed to Friedrichshain (eg Ostkreuz, 30 minutes) or Prenzlauer Berg (eg Schönhauser Allee, 45 minutes).

➜ The nearest U-Bahn station, Rudow, is about a 10-minute ride on bus X7 or bus 171 from the airport. From Rudow, the U7 takes you straight into town. This connection is useful if you're headed for Neukölln or Kreuzberg.

➜ All journeys cost €3.30 (tariff ABC).

➜ A cab ride to central Berlin averages €42 and takes 40 minutes to an hour.

From Hauptbahnhof

➜ Berlin's central train station is served by U-Bahn, S-Bahn, trams and buses.

➜ Taxi ranks are located outside the

north exit (Europaplatz)
and the south exit
(Washingtonplatz).

ZOB (Central Coach Station)

➡ Most long-haul buses
arrive at the **Zentraler
Omnibusbahnhof** (ZOB;
☎ 030-3010 0175; www.
iob-berlin.de; Masurenallee
4-6; **S** Messe/ICC Nord,
U Kaiserdamm) near the
trade fair grounds on the
western city edge.

➡ The closest U-Bahn
station is Kaiserdamm,
about 400m north and
served by the U2 which
travels straight through
the city centre. Tickets
cost €2.70 (Tariff AB).

➡ The nearest S-Bahn
station is Messe Süd/ICC,
about 200m east of ZOB.
It is served by the Ring-
bahn (circle line) S41/42
and handy for such
districts as Prenzlauer
Berg, Friedrichshain and
Neukölln. You need an AB
ticket (€2.70).

➡ Budget about €14 for
a taxi ride to the western
city centre and €22 to the
eastern city centre.

Getting Around

For information and trip
planning, see www.bvg.
de. Most single tickets

Tickets & Passes

➡ One ticket is valid for all forms of public transport.

➡ The network comprises fare zones A, B and C with tickets available for
zones AB, BC or ABC.

➡ AB tickets, valid for two hours, cover most city trips (interruptions and
transfers allowed, round-trips not). Exceptions: Potsdam and Schönefeld
Airport (ABC tariff).

➡ Children aged six to 14 qualify for reduced (*ermässigt*) rates; kids under six
travel free.

➡ One-day passes (*Tageskarte*; €7) are valid for unlimited rides on all forms of
public transport until 3am the following day. The group day pass (*Kleingruppen-
Tageskarte*; €17.30) is valid for up to five people travelling together.

➡ Buy tickets from bus drivers, vending machines at U- or S-Bahn stations
and aboard trams, station offices, and news kiosks sporting the yellow BVG
logo. Some vending machines accept debit cards. Bus drivers and tram vending machines only take cash.

➡ Single tickets, except those bought from bus drivers and in trams, must be
validated before boarding.

➡ On-the-spot fine for travelling without a valid ticket: €40.

➡ A range of travel passes offer good value.

need to be validated before or upon boarding.

U-Bahn

➡ Lines (referred to as U1, U2 etc) operate from 4am until about 12.30am and throughout the night on Friday, Saturday and public holidays (all lines except the U4 and U55).

➡ From Sunday to Thursday, night buses take over in the interim.

S-Bahn & Train

➡ S-Bahn trains (S1, S2 etc) operate from 4am to 12.30am and all night on Friday, Saturday and public holidays.

➡ Destinations further afield are served by RB and RE trains. You'll need an ABC or **Deutsche Bahn** (☏01806 99 66 33;

www.bahn.de) ticket to use these trains.

Bus

➡ Buses run frequently between 4.30am and 12.30am.

➡ Night buses (designated N19, N23 etc) take over after 12.30am.

➡ MetroBuses (designated M19, M41 etc) operate 24/7.

➡ Tickets bought from bus drivers don't need to be validated.

Tram

➡ Trams (*Strassenbahn*) operate almost exclusively in the eastern districts.

➡ Those designated M1, M2 etc, run 24/7.

Bicycle

➡ Many hotels and hostels have guest bikes. Alternatively, rental stations abound.

➡ Bicycles may be taken aboard designated U-Bahn and S-Bahn carriages (look for the bicycle logo) as well as on night buses (Sunday to Thursday only) and trams. You need a separate bicycle ticket called a *Fahrradkarte* (€1.90).

➡ The websites www.bbbike.de and www.vmz-info.de are handy for route planning.

Taxi

➡ You can order a taxi by phone, flag one down or pick one up at a rank. At night, cars often line up outside theatres, clubs and other venues.

➡ Flag fall is €3.90, then it's €2 per kilometre up to 7km and €1.50 for each additional kilometre.

➡ Credit or debit card surcharge is €1.50. Tip about 10%.

➡ The *Kurzstreckentarif* (short-trip rate) lets you ride in a cab for up to 2km for €5 provided you flag down a moving taxi and request this rate

Late-Night & Sunday Shopping

➡ One handy feature of Berlin culture is the *Spätkauf* (*Späti* in local vernacular), which are small neighbourhood stores stocked with the basics and open from early evening until 2am or later.

➡ Some supermarkets stay open until midnight; a few are even 24 hours.

➡ Shops and supermarkets in major train stations (Hauptbahnhof, Ostbahnhof, Friedrichstrasse) are open late and on Sunday.

before the driver has activated the regular meter.

Essential Information

Business Hours

Many boutiques and smaller shops don't open until noon and close at 6pm or 7pm.

Bars 7pm to 1am or later

Clubs 11pm to 5am or later

Restaurants 11am to 11pm

Shops 10am to 8pm Monday to Saturday

Supermarkets 8am to 8pm or later; some 24 hours

Discount Cards

Berlin Welcome Card (www.berlin-welcome-card.de) Valid for unlimited public transport for one adult and up to three children under 14 for up to 50% discount to 200 sights, attractions and tours; available for up to six days.

CityTourCard (www.citytourcard.com) Similar to the Berlin Welcome Card but a bit cheaper and with fewer discounts.

Museumspass Berlin Buys admission to the permanent exhibits of about 50 museums for three consecutive opening days. It sells for €24 (concession €12) at tourist offices and participating museums.

Electricity

230V/50Hz

Emergency

Ambulance (☎112)

Fire Department (☎112)

Police (☎110)

Money

➜ The easiest and quickest way to obtain cash is from an ATM (*Geldautomat*). Check with your bank for fees and daily withdrawal limits.

➜ Cash is king in Germany.

➜ Credit cards are becoming more widely accepted (especially in hotels and upmarket shops and restaurants) but it's best to enquire first.

➜ Report lost or stolen cards to the central number ☎116 116.

Public Holidays

Shops, banks and public and private offices are closed on the following *gesetzliche Feiertage* (public holidays):

Neujahrstag (New Year's Day) 1 January

Ostern (Easter) March/April; Good Friday, Easter Sunday and Easter Monday

Christi Himmelfahrt (Ascension Day) Forty days after Easter, always on a Thursday

Maifeiertag (Labour Day) 1 May

Dos & Don'ts

➡ Do say *'Guten Tag'* when entering a business.

➡ Do state your last name at the start of a phone call.

➡ Do bring a small gift or flowers when invited to a home-cooked meal.

➡ Do bag your own groceries in supermarkets. And quickly!

➡ Don't be late for appointments and dinner invitations.

➡ Don't assume you can pay by credit card, especially when eating out.

Pfingsten (Whitsun/ Pentecost Sunday and Monday) May/June

Tag der Deutschen Einheit (Day of German Unity) 3 October

Reformationstag (Reformation Day; Brandenburg state only) 31 October

Weihnachtstag (Christmas Day) 25 December

Zweiter Weihnachtstag (Boxing Day) 26 December

Telephone

➡ Berlin's city code is ☎030; Germany's country code is ☎49.

➡ Mobile phones operate on GSM900/1800.

➡ Local SIM cards can be used in unlocked European and Australian phones.

➡ US multiband phones also work in Germany.

Toilets

➡ German toilets are sit-down affairs; men are expected to sit when peeing.

➡ Toilets in malls, clubs, beer gardens etc often have an attendant who expects a tip of around €0.50.

Tourist Information

Visit Berlin (www.visit berlin.de), the Berlin tourist board, operates five walk-in offices, info desks at the airports, and a **call centre** (☎030-2500 2333; ⊙9am-7pm Mon-Fri, 10am-6pm Sat, 10am-2pm Sun) whose multilingual staff field general questions and make hotel and ticket bookings.

Brandenburger Tor (Brandenburger Tor, south wing, Pariser Platz; ⊙9.30am-7pm Apr-Oct, to 6pm Nov-Mar; Ⓢ Brandenburger Tor, Ⓤ Brandenburger Tor)

Hauptbahnhof (Hauptbahnhof, Europaplatz entrance, ground fl; ⊙8am-10pm; Ⓢ Hauptbahnhof, Ⓡ Hauptbahnhof)

Europa-Center (Tauentzienstrasse 9, Europa-Center, ground fl; ⊙10am-8pm Mon-Sat; 🚌100, 200, Ⓤ Kurfürstendamm)

Rankestrasse (cnr Rankestrasse & Kurfürstendamm; ⊙10am-6pm Apr-Oct, to 4pm Nov-Mar; 🚌100, 200, Ⓤ Kurfürstendamm)

TV Tower (Panoramastrasse 1a, TV Tower, ground fl; ⊙10am-6pm Apr-Oct, to 4pm Nov-Mar; 🚌100, 200, TXL, Ⓤ Alexanderplatz, Ⓢ Alexanderplatz)

Travellers with Disabilities

➡ Access ramps and/ or lifts are available in

many public buildings, including train stations, museums, concert halls and cinemas.

➡ Most buses, trains and trams are wheelchair-accessible and many U-Bahn and S-Bahn stations are equipped with ramps or lifts. For trip-planning assistance, contact **BVG** (📞030-19449; www.bvg.de).

➡ **Rollstuhlpannendienst** (📞0177 833 5773; www.rollstuhlpannendienst.de; 🕓24hr) provides 24-hour wheelchair repairs and rentals.

➡ Download Lonely Planet's free *Accessible Travel* guide from http://lptravel.to/AccessibleTravel.

Visas

➡ EU nationals need only their national identity card or passport to enter Germany.

➡ Citizens of Australia, Canada, Israel, Japan, New Zealand, Switzerland and the US are among those who need only a valid passport (no visa) if entering as tourists for stays under three months.

➡ Nationals from most other countries need a Schengen Visa to enter Germany. For details, check with a German consulate in your country.

Language

It's easy to pronounce German because almost all sounds are also found in English – just read our pronunciation guides as if they were English and you'll be understood.

In German, word stress falls mostly on the first syllable – in our pronunciation guides the stressed syllable is indicated with italics.

Note that German has polite and informal forms for 'you' (*Sie* and *du* respectively). When addressing people you don't know well, use the polite form. In this language guide, polite forms are used, unless you see (pol/inf) which indicates we've given both options. Also note that (m/f) indicates masculine and feminine forms.

To enhance your trip with a phrasebook, visit **lonelyplanet.com**.

Basics

Hello.
Guten Tag.   goo·ten taak

Goodbye.
Auf   owf
Wiedersehen.   vee·der·zey·en

How are you? (pol/inf)
Wie geht es   vee gayt es
Ihnen/dir?   ee·nen/deer

Fine, thanks.
Danke, gut.   dang·ke goot

Please.
Bitte.   bi·te

Thank you.
Danke.   dang·ke

Excuse me.
Entschuldigung.   ent·shul·di·gung

Sorry.
Entschuldigung.   ent·shul·di·gung

Yes./No.
Ja./Nein.   yah/nain

Do you speak (English)?
Sprechen Sie   shpre·khen zee
Englisch?   eng·lish

I (don't) understand.
Ich verstehe   ikh fer·shtay·e
(nicht).   (nikht)

Eating & Drinking

I'm a vegetarian. (m/f)
Ich bin Vegetarier/   ikh bin ve·ge·tah·ri·er/
Vegetarierin.   ve·ge·tah·ri·e·in

Cheers!
Prost!   prawst

That was delicious!
Das war sehr   das vahr zair
lecker!   le·ker

Please bring the bill.
Die Rechnung,   dee rekh·nung
bitte.   bi·te

I'd like ...
Ich möchte ...   ikh merkh·te ...

a coffee   *einen Kaffee*   ai·nen ka·fay

a glass of *ein Glas*   ain glas
wine   *Wein*   wain

a table   *einen Tisch*   ai·nen tish
for two   *für zwei*   für tsvai
               Personen   per·zaw·nen

two beers *zwei Bier*   tsvai beer

Shopping

I'd like to buy ...
Ich möchte ...   ikh merkh·te ...
kaufen.   kow·fen

May I look at it?
Können Sie es   ker·nen zee es
mir zeigen?   meer *tsai*·gen

How much is it?
Wie viel kostet das?   vee feel *kos*·tet das

That's too expensive.
Das ist zu teuer.   das ist tsoo *toy*·er

Can you lower the price?
Können Sie mit   ker·nen zee mit
dem Preis   dem prais
heruntergehen?   he·*run*·ter·gay·en

There's a mistake in the bill.
Da ist ein Fehler in   dah ist ain *fay*·ler in
der Rechnung.   dair *rekh*·nung

Emergencies

Help!
Hilfe!   *hil*·fe

Call a doctor!
Rufen Sie   roo·fen zee
einen Arzt!   *ai*·nen artst

Call the police!
Rufen Sie   roo·fen zee
die Polizei!   dee po·li·*tsai*

I'm lost.
Ich habe   ikh *hah*·be
mich verirrt.   mikh fer·*irt*

I'm ill.
Ich bin krank.   ikh bin krangk

Where's the toilet?
Wo ist die Toilette?   vo ist dee to·a·le·te

Time & Numbers

What time is it?
Wie spät ist es?   vee shpayt ist es

It's (10) o'clock.
Es ist (zehn) Uhr.   es ist (tsayn) oor

morning	*Morgen*	mor·gen
afternoon	*Nach-mittag*	nahkh·mi·tahk
evening	*Abend*	ah·bent

yesterday	*gestern*	ges·tern
today	*heute*	hoy·te
tomorrow	*morgen*	mor·gen

1	*eins*	ains
2	*zwei*	tsvai
3	*drei*	drai
4	*vier*	feer
5	*fünf*	fünf
6	*sechs*	zeks
7	*sieben*	zee·ben
8	*acht*	akht
9	*neun*	noyn
10	*zehn*	tsayn
100	*hundert*	hun·dert
1000	*tausend*	tow·sent

Transport & Directions

Where's ...?
Wo ist ...?   vaw ist ...

What's the address?
Wie ist die   vee ist dee
Adresse?   a·dre·se

Can you show me (on the map)?
Können Sie mir   ker·nen zee es meer
(auf der Karte)   (owf dair kar·te)
zeigen?   tsai·gen

I want to go to ...
Ich mochte   ikh merkh·te
nach ... fahren.   nahkh ... fah·ren

What time does it leave?
Wann fährt es ab?   van fairt es ap

What time does it arrive?
Wann kommt   van komt
es an?   es an

Does it stop at ...?
Hält es in ...?   helt es in ...

I want to get off here.
Ich mochte hier   ikh merkh·te heer
aussteigen.   ows·shtai·gen

Behind the Scenes

Send Us Your Feedback

We love to hear from travellers – your comments help make our books better. We read every word, and we guarantee that your feedback goes straight to the authors. Visit **lonelyplanet.com/contact** to submit your updates and suggestions.

Note: We may edit, reproduce and incorporate your comments in Lonely Planet products such as guidebooks, websites and digital products, so let us know if you don't want your comments reproduced or your name acknowledged. For a copy of our privacy policy visit lonelyplanet.com/privacy.

Andrea's Thanks

Big heartfelt thanks to all the wonderful people who supplied me with tips, insights, information, ideas and encouragement, including (in no particular order): Henrik Tidefjaerd, Barbara Woolsey, Frank Engster, Claudia Scheffler, Ubin Eoh, Patricia Kurowski, Shachar and Dorit Elkanati, Renate Freiling, Bernd Olsson, Christian Tänzler, Nicole Röbel, Julia Rautenberg, Claudi Sult and many more too numerous to mention here.

Acknowledgements

Cover photograph: Spree River, Jon Arnold/AWL©.

This Book

This 5th edition of Lonely Planet's *Pocket Berlin* guidebook was researched and written by Andrea Schulte-Peevers. She also wrote the previous two editions. This guidebook was produced by the following:

Destination Editor
Gemma Graham

Product Editor
Kathryn Rowan

Senior Cartographer
Valentina Kremenchutskaya

Book Designer
Mazzy Prinsep

Assisting Editors Imogen Bannister, Gabrielle Innes, Gabrielle Stefanos, Saralinda Turner

Cover Researcher
Naomi Parker

Thanks to Gerry Bell, David Halliday, Andi Jones, Lauren Keith, Catherine Naghten, Claire Naylor, Karyn Noble, Alison Lyall, Kirsten Rawlings, Charles Taylor, Tony Wheeler

Index

See also separate subindexes for:

⊗ **Eating p189**

⊝ **Drinking p190**

✪ **Entertainment p190**

⊕ **Shopping p191**

Our Writer

Andrea Schulte-Peevers

Born and raised in Germany and educated in London and at UCLA, Andrea has travelled the distance to the moon and back in her visits to some 75 countries. She has earned her living as a professional travel writer for over two decades and authored or contributed to nearly 100 Lonely Planet titles as well as to newspapers, magazines and websites around the world. She also works as a travel consultant, translator and editor. Andrea's destination expertise is especially strong when it comes to Germany, Dubai and the UAE, Crete and the Caribbean Islands. She makes her home in Berlin.

Published by Lonely Planet Global Limited
CRN 554153
5th edition – Feb 2017
ISBN 978 1 78657 233 2
© Lonely Planet 2017 Photographs © as indicated 2017
10 9 8 7 6 5 4 3
Printed in Malaysia